The Fujifilm X-T2

Rico Pfirstinger studied communications and has been working as a journalist, publicist, and photographer since the mid-'80s. He has written numerous books on a diverse range of topics, from computing technology to digital desktop publishing to sled dog racing. He worked as the department head of special assignments for Hubert Burda Media in Munich, Germany, where he also served as chief editor for a winter sports website.

After eight years as a freelance film critic in Los Angeles, Rico now lives in Germany and devotes his time to digital photography and compact camera systems.

Rico writes the popular X-Pert Corner blog and leads workshops called Fuji X Secrets where he offers tips and tricks on using the Fujifilm X-series cameras.

Rico Pfirstinger

The Fujifilm X-T2

120 X-Pert Tips to Get the Most
Out of Your Camera

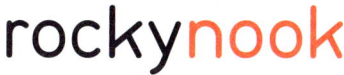

The Fujifilm X-T2: 120 X-Pert Tips to Get the Most Out of Your Camera
Rico Pfirstinger

Project editor: Maggie Yates
Project manager: Lisa Brazieal
Marketing manager: Jessica Tiernan
Copyeditor: Maggie Yates
Translation: Rico Pfirstinger
Layout and type: Petra Strauch
Cover design: Rebecca Cowlin
Indexer: Maggie Yates

ISBN: 978-1-68198-222-9
1st Edition (3rd printing, April 2018)
© 2017 Rico Pfirstinger
All images © Rico Pfirstinger unless otherwise noted

Rocky Nook, Inc.
1010 B Street, Suite 350
San Rafael, CA 94901
U.S.A.

www.rockynook.com

Distributed in the U.S. by Ingram Publisher Services
Distributed in the UK and Europe by Publishers Group UK

Library of Congress Control Number: 2016950251

Printed in the U.S.A.

Table of Contents

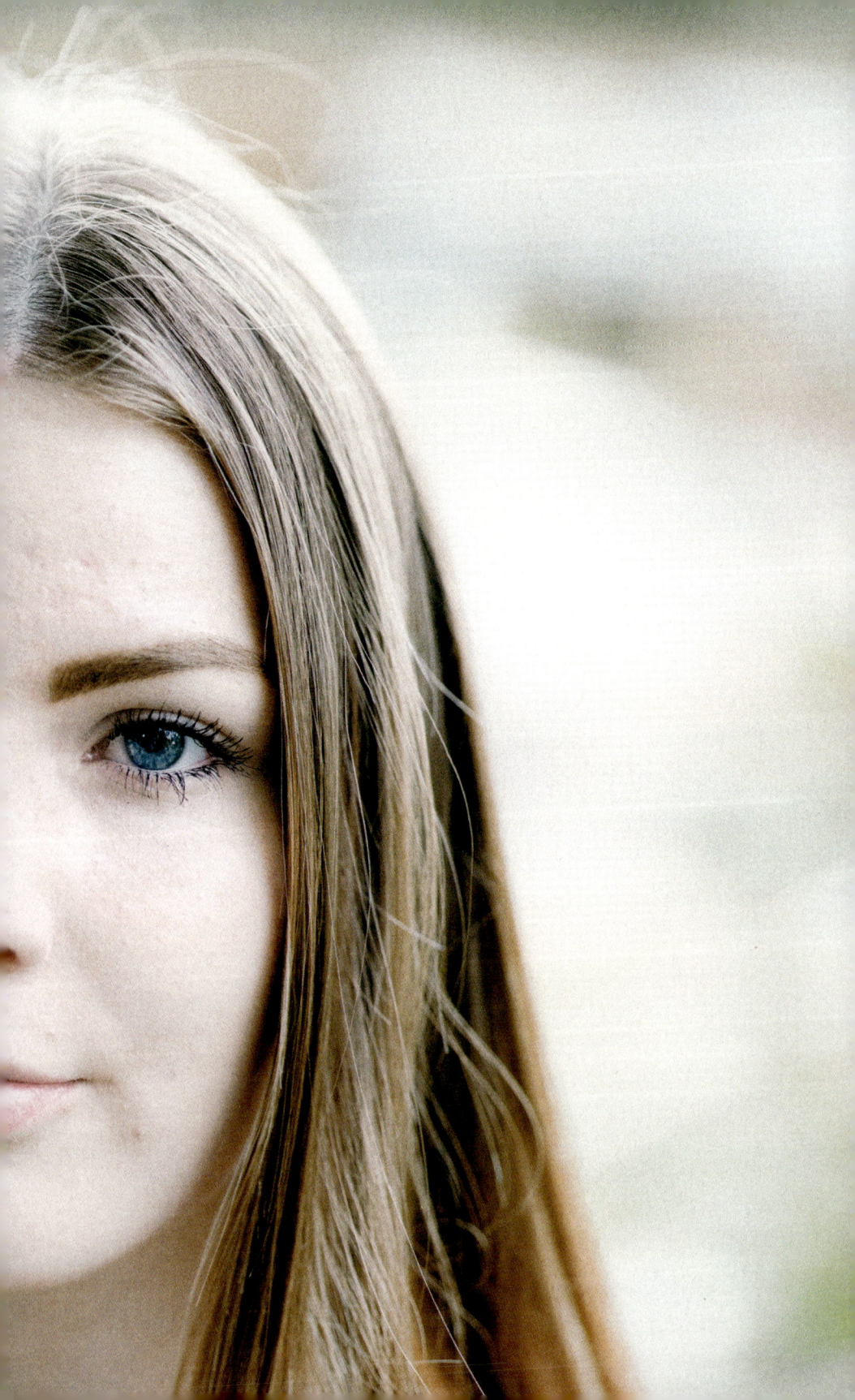

1. YOUR X-T2 SYSTEM

To start off, here's a brief overview of the buttons and controls on your Fujifilm X-T2:

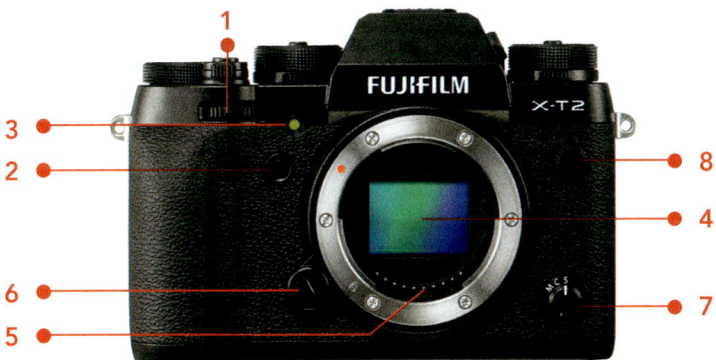

Fig. 1: **X-T2 frontal view:** front command dial with integrated button (1), Fn button (2), AF assist lamp/self-timer indicator lamp (3), X-Trans sensor (4), electronic lens contacts (5), lens release button (6), focus selector (7), flash sync connector (8)

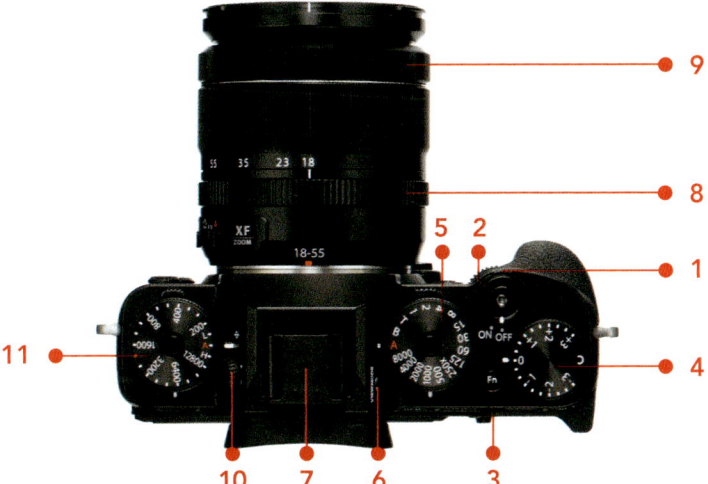

Fig. 2: **X-T2 top view (with XF18–55mmF2.8–4 R LM OIS):** on/off switch (1), shutter release button (2), Fn button (3), exposure compensation dial (4), shutter speed dial with stacked metering mode selection dial (5), view mode button (6), hot shoe (7), aperture ring (8), focus ring (9), diopter adjustment dial (10), ISO dial with stacked DRIVE mode dial (11)

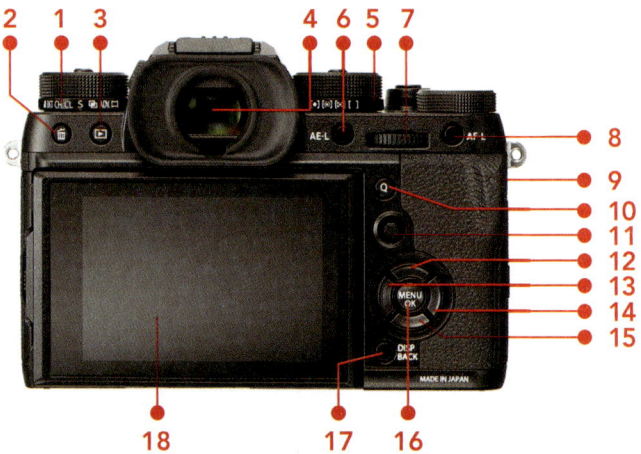

Fig. 3: **X-T2 rear view:** DRIVE mode dial (1), delete ("trash") button (2), playback button (3), viewfinder (4), metering mode selection dial (5), AE-L button/Fn button (6), rear command dial with integrated button (7), AF-L button/Fn button (8), status indicator lamp (9), Q button for Quick menu (10), focus stick with integrated button (11), upper selector/Fn button (12), left selector/Fn button (13), right selector/Fn button (14), lower selector/Fn button (15), MENU/OK button (16), DISP/BACK button (17), LCD monitor (18)

1.1 THE BASICS (1): THINGS YOU SHOULD KNOW ABOUT YOUR CAMERA

RTFM! Read The Fuji Manual! It is included with your camera.	**TIP 1**

In case you have misplaced your user manual, or if you want to update to a newer edition of the manual, you can click this link [01] to obtain downloadable PDF versions in all supported languages. You will also find supplementary material that covers new features and changes based on firmware updates.

Please do yourself a big favor and thoroughly study this manual in order to get acquainted with the different functions of your X-T2, and don't forget that your lenses come with a user manual, as well. This book doesn't replace the X-T2 camera manual; it serves as an *enhancement* to the manual, and offers valuable tips and background information about how to use the various features and functions of the X-T2 and make the most of your equipment.

Get a few **spare batteries**. You can buy suitable batteries from Fujifilm or from a third party.	**TIP 2**

The X-T2 is quite a compact camera, which means that the rechargeable battery is also rather small. Depending on how you use your camera, a fully charged battery will last for 250 to 400 shots.

I recommend setting the camera to Boost Mode (SET UP > POWER MANAGEMENT > PERFORMANCE > BOOST) in order to secure maximum autofocus and overall performance.

Please note:

- Unlike previous models, the X-T2 features an accurate battery indicator with five bars and a percentage display.

- In shooting mode, the percentage display is only available in the INFO display. To activate the INFO display, (repeatedly) press the DISP/BACK button until the INFO display appears. In playback mode, the percentage indicator is also available in the INFO display, which can be accessed with the DISP/BACK button *or* by pressing the upper selector key to cycle through two extended image information pages.

- When the battery indicator shows one remaining red bar, it's almost time to replace the battery.

Your X-T2 is using NP-W126S rechargeable batteries. This type of battery is also used in Fujifilm's X-Pro1, X-E1, X-E2, X-T1, X-T10, X-M1, X-A1, X-A2, X-A3, and X-A10 cameras, and can be interchanged between these models.

You can also use older NP-W126 type batteries. The only difference between the regular and the S type batteries is their ability to manage heat. For high-performance applications such as long 4K video recordings in a hot environment, the newer NP-W126S type, which is more efficient at managing heat, may be favorable. However, if you already own a bunch of older NP-W126 batteries, there's no reason not to use them in your X-T2.

You can obtain NP-W126S batteries from Fujifilm, or you can use compatible products from a variety of third-party vendors. Sadly, not all aftermarket batteries offer the same quality and capacity as the more expensive Fujifilm batteries.

You may experience inaccurate battery life displays with third-party offerings, and the camera may unexpectedly switch off with an empty battery even though the indicator shows there was some power left. To avoid such trouble, use original Fujifilm NP-W126 or NP-W126S batteries.

If you store your camera for several days (or longer) without a charged battery, the X-T2's built-in emergency power source may run out of juice, and all camera and user settings will reset to factory conditions.

Get a suitable **battery charger** and a **travel adapter**.	**TIP 3**

Along with spare batteries, the aftermarket also offers chargers that work with regular power outlets, USB ports, or a car's cigarette lighter jack. This way, you can charge your batteries not only at home or in your hotel room, but also on your computer's USB port or when you are traveling in a car or plane.

While traveling, don't forget that different countries use different formats for power outlets, so you may want to carry a suitable travel adapter. A particularly small and practical solution is the Apple World Travel Adapter Kit [02]. It contains adapters for North America, Japan, China, the United Kingdom, Continental Europe, Korea, Australia, and Hong Kong. The adapters connect directly to the charger that comes with your X-T2 (no cable required). You can also use them with chargers for your Apple device (iPhone, iPad, MacBook, etc.).

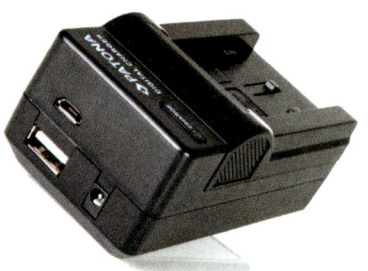

Fig. 4:
Some third-party chargers can get their power from more than one source, such as power outlets, USB ports, and car cigarette lighter jacks.

As an alternative to external battery chargers, the battery can also be charged inside the X-T2 via the camera's USB port. Use a USB 2 or USB 3 micro cable to connect the X-T2 to pretty much any power source with a USB port, such as your laptop or your cell phone charger.

| TIP 4 | Make sure that your camera and lenses are running with the latest **firmware**. |

Fujifilm keeps improving the firmware of the X-T2 and XF/ XC lenses.

- In order to check which firmware version is installed in your camera and lens, switch on the camera while pressing and holding the DISP/BACK button.

- Use this link [03] to find and download the latest firmware versions for your camera and lenses. There, you can also find current versions of Fuji's application software, such as RAW File Converter EX.

- A step-by-step video guide illustrating the firmware upgrade process is available here [04]. MacOS users can find detailed firmware download instructions here [05]. Windows users can use this link [06].

| TIP 5 | Things to remember when **updating your firmware**: |

- Always use card slot number 1 for firmware updates.

- If you can't find a new firmware version on Fuji's firmware update page, there's a good chance that your web browser is still caching an older version of this page. In this case, either delete your browser cache or force your browser to reload the webpage from the server.

- Make sure that your computer doesn't change the name of firmware files you download due to naming conflicts caused by previous firmware versions that are still residing in your download folder. The correct file name of the camera firmware for your X-T2 is always FWUP0010.DAT.

- Make sure your battery is fully charged when updating your firmware.

- Always copy new firmware files for your camera or lenses into the top directory of your SD memory card, and always use cards that have been freshly formatted in your camera. After you have copied the firmware to the card, make sure to properly unmount the card from your computer before removing it.

- If you want to update the firmware for a specific lens, make sure that lens is attached to the camera when you initiate the update process.

- To start the update process for your camera or a lens, switch on the camera while pressing and holding the DISP/BACK button and follow the instructions on the screen.

- Never switch the camera off during the update process. The camera will tell you when the update is complete. Only then can you safely switch it off.

If the firmware of your camera or lens needs to be updated due to compatibility issues, the camera may alert you of this when you switch it on. If that's the case, download the new firmware from the website links provided in tip 4 and update your camera and/or lens.

Use fast **memory cards** with at least 80 MB/s write speed.	TIP 6

Turbo-charge your camera and its built-in buffer memory by using the fastest UHS-I and UHS-II memory cards available. SanDisk, Lexar and Toshiba offer cards with nominal write speeds of 80 MB/s or higher.

The X-T2 also supports the superfast UHS-II standard, which offers transmission speeds of up to 300 MB/s. Unlike the X-Pro2, UHS-II is available in both SD card slots of your X-T2.

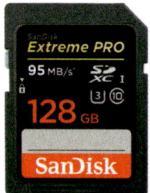

Fig. 5:
Fast **SanDisk Extreme Pro** SD memory cards with a 95 MB/s read and write speed are popular workhorses for many serious X-series users.

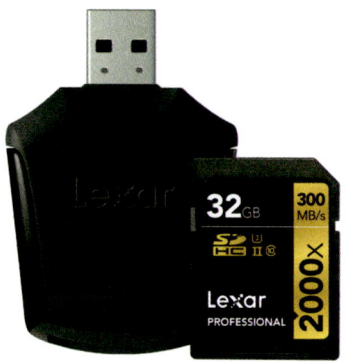

Fig. 6:
For maximum performance, I recommend you use lightning-fast UHS-II cards, like a **Lexar Professional 2000x,** Toshiba Exceria Pro, or SanDisk Extreme Pro UHS-II.

TIP 7	Working with **Dual Card Slots:**

Your X-T2 offers two SD card slots numbered "1" and "2". This means that you can use two SD cards at the same time.

Please note:

- The primary SD card slot of your X-T2 is always slot #1. If you are only working with a single SD card, always put it in this slot.

- Firmware upgrades are only supported in slot #1.

- Both slots support UHS-II, making them suitable for very fast memory cards such as *Lexar Professional 2000x, Toshiba Exceria Pro,* or *SanDisk Extreme Pro UHS-II (280 MB/s).*

Using two memory cards at the same time gives you three different options to configure how image data is transferred to your SD cards. To do so, select SET UP > SAVE DATA SET-UP > CARD SLOT SETTING (STILL IMAGE) and pick one of the following options:

- **SEQUENTIAL:** In this default mode, the camera saves all image data (RAW and JPEG) to a manually selected card slot. To change the slot, choose SET UP > SAVE DATA SET-UP > SWITCH SLOT (SEQUENTIAL).

- **BACKUP:** In this mode, the X-T2 is sending all image data (RAW and JPEG) to both slots at the same time, creating a backup copy that can be useful when one of the cards gets lost or suffers data loss. In this mode, the overall data transfer rate is limited by the slower of the two cards that are in use. This can become a performance issue in situations that require many images being taken with high burst rates while shooting FINE+RAW, so make sure that the cards in both slots are equally fast.

- **RAW/JPEG:** This setting splits the image data up by saving RAW files to slot #1 and JPEGs to slot #2, so this setting is only useful when you are shooting FINE+RAW or NORMAL+RAW. If you shoot RAW-only or JPEG-only, RAW/JPEG mode turns into BACKUP mode, saving your RAW or JPEG data to both cards at the same time.

I always recommend shooting FINE+RAW. If you follow this advice, selecting RAW/JPEG mode (and using the fastest UHS-II cards available in slots #1 and #2, respectively) will give you the best camera performance in terms of continuous burst rates.

However, RAW/JPEG data save mode also has its quirks:

- Splitting up RAW and JPEG image data to slots #1 and #2 only works in regular shooting mode (i.e., when you take a new picture), not when you are using the camera's built-in RAW converter to create a JPEG from a RAW file on card #1. JPEGs generated from RAWs on card #1 are also saved on card #1 (the RAW card) instead of card #2 (the JPEG card).

■ In playback mode, the X-T2 will display small HD-sized JPEG images that are embedded in the RAW files on card #1 instead of showing the full-resolution JPEGs on card #2. To access the full-resolution JPEGs (e.g., in order to zoom in and check critical focus), you have to manually switch slots in playback mode by pressing and holding the playback button until the camera confirms the switch. Sadly, the camera will revert back to the other card as soon as you take another picture, so you'll have to go through the motions of switching slots in playback mode each time you take another shot.

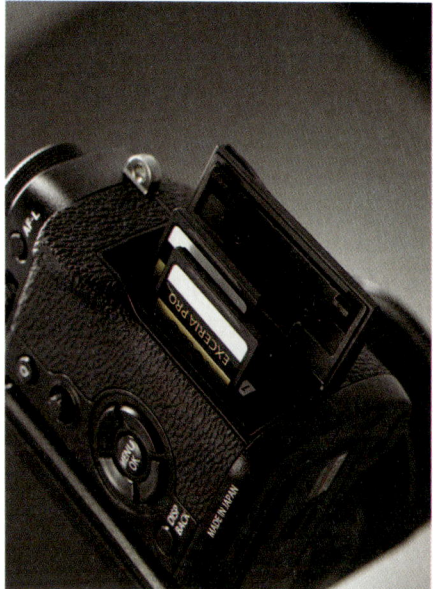

Fig. 7: Your X-T2 can work with **two SD memory cards at the same time.** For maximum performance, you should use fast UHS-II cards (such as the Lexar Professional 2000x with 300 MB/s).

Your camera is automatically numbering your images. With a
little trick, you can **reset the frame counter** and even assign a
new starting number.   **TIP 8**

Make sure that you only use a single SD card in slot #1. Then
follow these steps to reset the image counter to zero:

■ First select SET UP > SAVE DATA SET-UP > FRAME NO. >
RENEW, then format the SD card with SET UP > USER SET-
TING > FORMAT > SLOT 1 and take a picture. The frame
counter will start from zero.

■ To avoid another automatic image counter reset when
you are reformatting an SD card, select SET UP > SAVE
DATA SET-UP > FRAME NO. > CONTINUOUS.

You can assign pretty much any number as the camera's
new frame-counter starting number. The method is similar,
but involves an extra step in your computer. Again, only use
a single SD card in slot #1:

■ Select SET UP > SAVE DATA SET-UP > FRAME NO. > RENEW,
then format the SD card with SET UP > USER SETTING >
FORMAT > SLOT 1 and take a picture. The frame counter
will start from zero.

■ Remove the SD card from your camera and insert it in your
computer. Locate your image (for example DSCF0001.
JPG or DSCF0001.RAF) in the DCIM folder and change
the frame-number portion of the file name (0001) to the
number you'd like to use as your new starting point. For
example, you can change the file name to DSCF2000.JPG.

■ Properly unmount and remove the SD card from your
computer and put the card back into your camera. Now
take another picture. The camera will use the modified
frame number as a starting point. In our example, the
new image file's name would be DSCF2001.

■ To avoid another automatic frame-counter reset when you are reformatting an SD card, select SET UP > SAVE DATA SET-UP > FRAME NO. > CONTINUOUS.

Please note that the X-T2 doesn't feature an internal shutter actuations counter. Image file numbers are no indication of the actual number of shots that have been taken with a particular camera and aren't a suitable measurement to gauge the wear and tear of the camera's mechanical shutter.

| TIP 9 | Use **Boost mode!** |

In its default setting, the X-T2 operates with limited perfor-mance in order to conserve power. To enjoy the camera's full capabilities, it's necessary to select SET UP > POWER MANAGEMENT > PERFORMANCE > BOOST, or assign Boost mode to one of the camera's eight Fn buttons.

If you have the Vertical Power Booster Grip attached to your X-T2, Boost mode is set with the switch on the back of the grip. Since the X-T2 consumes more power in Boost mode, it's even more important to always have replacement batteries at hand.

Without the Vertical Power Booster Grip, Boost mode offers better autofocus performance (minimum reaction time of 0.06 seconds from 0.08 seconds) and a higher frame rate in the electronic real-time live view (100 fps instead of 60 fps).

In concert with the Vertical Power Booster Grip, Boost mode also reduces the shooting interval (from 0.19 to 0.17 seconds), the shutter time lag (from 0.05 to 0.045 sec-onds) and the live view blackout time between burst shots (from 0.130 to 0.114 seconds). Last but not least, it offers a maximum burst rate of 11 fps with the mechanical shutter in continuous shooting mode CH.

Click here [07] to learn more about the Vertical Power Booster Grip's features and benefits.

Important: When Boost mode is *off,* the camera will enter an energy saving mode after approximately 10 seconds of user inactivity. This results in a dramatic reduction of the live view's frame rate. As soon as a button is pushed or a dial is turned, the live view goes back to normal.

Keep the **camera sensor** clean!	**TIP 10**

Sooner or later, all cameras with interchangeable lenses get dust or dirt on the sensor. This manifests as spots on your image, especially in photos taken at small apertures. You can prevent this from happening by taking measures to avoid sensor dust as much as possible. You can clean dust by using your camera's built-in cleaning mechanism:

■ Select SET UP > USER SETTING > SENSOR CLEANING > OK to activate the built-in cleaning mechanism that helps loosen dust particles. By default, this mechanism will be employed when you switch *off* the camera. I recommend setting the camera to also automatically activate this mechanism when the X-T2 is switched *on:* to do this, select SET UP > USER SETTING > SENSOR CLEANING > WHEN SWITCHED ON > ON.

In addition to that, it's sensible to adhere to a regiment that avoids exposing the camera to dust and dirt:

■ Never leave the camera without a lens or its protective body cap.

■ Don't exchange lenses in dusty environments.

■ When exchanging lenses, always hold the camera with the open lens mount pointed downward—never upward.

■ When you attach a new lens, make sure the rear glass of the lens is clean and free of dust particles. Otherwise, dust from the lens could travel to the sensor.

■ Never touch the sensor!

Fig. 8: **Dust spots** on the sensor made visible: this sensor badly needs cleaning.

<table>
<tr><td>**TIP 11**</td><td>**Do-it-yourself sensor cleaning** for tough sensor spots:</td></tr>
</table>

When the built-in sensor-cleaning function doesn't do a proper job, you have three basic options for cleaning the sensor by yourself:

■ Touchless cleaning
■ Dry cleaning
■ Wet cleaning

Touchless cleaning involves using a blower, like the *Giotto's Rocket-air Blower,* to rid the sensor of dust particles. An important feature of such devices is a filter in the intake valve that prevents contaminated (dusty) air from being blown against the sensor.

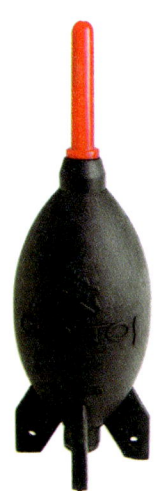

Fig. 9: Touchless sensor cleaning: **Rocket-air Blower**

Important: Don't use compressed air from aerosol cans that contain propellants. Particles could hit the sensor like tiny projectiles and damage it!

A popular means to **dry clean** the sensor is the Pentax Sensor Cleaning Kit. The sticky head of this funny-looking cleaning device picks up dust and dirt from the sensor surface and transfers it to sticky paper sheets that are included with the product.

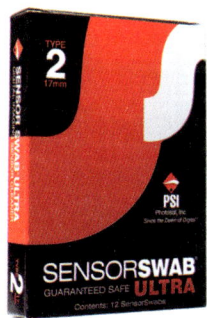

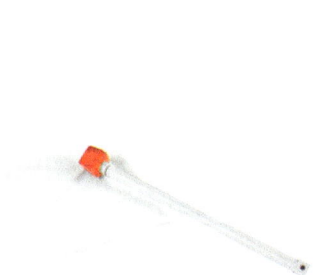

Fig. 10:
Dry cleaning:
Pentax Sensor Cleaning Kit

Fig. 11:
Wet cleaning:
sensor swab from Photographic Solutions

Tough sensor dirt (like water or oil stains) requires wet cleaning with a *sensor swab*. Suitable products are offered by companies likes *Photographic Solutions* and *Visible Dust*. They consist of wipers that are wetted with special cleaning fluids (such as *Eclipse*). Wipe one side of the swab from left to right over the full width of the sensor, and then from right to left with the other side of the swab. Your X-T2 requires swabs that match APS-C-sized sensors. At Photographic Solutions, this translates into product size number 2.

Inexpensive and effective alternatives to products from Visible Dust or Photographic Solutions are APS-C-sized swabs from the Asian brand VSGO.

There's a small chance that the spots are caused by dust particles enclosed *behind* the protective surface of the sensor. If some spots simply won't go away, the camera needs to be serviced by Fujifilm. In some countries the first sensor cleaning is even free of charge.

1.2 THE BASICS (2): THINGS YOU SHOULD KNOW ABOUT YOUR LENSES

Your camera is compatible with the following native X-mount lenses:

- Fujinon XF lenses (prime and zoom lenses)

- Fujinon XC lenses (compact, more affordable lenses)

- Zeiss Touit X-mount lenses (primes)

Confused about which lens category does what? Here's the low-down as of November, 2016:

- Fujinon zoom lenses (except for the XF16–55mmF2.8 lens) feature an optical image stabilizer (OIS).

- Fujinon XF lenses (with the exception of the XF27mmF2.8 pancake lens) and Zeiss Touit lenses feature an aperture ring.

- XC lenses don't feature an aperture ring. With these lenses, the aperture is set using the camera's command dial.

- Fujinon XF and XC lenses (with the exception of the XF56mm APD prime lens) and the three Zeiss Touit lenses support fast phase detection autofocus (PDAF) with the camera's central AF frames. However, lacking adequate firmware updates, the autofocus performance of the Touits cannot keep up with Fujifilm's own lenses.

- Fujinon XF lenses offer LMO (lens modulation optimizer) support. The LMO mitigates undesirable optical effects such as diffraction, which occurs when a lens is stopped-down to a small aperture.

- Zeiss Touit lenses and Fujinon XC lenses do *not* support the LMO.

■ As of November, 2016, there are six lenses that support a particularly fast version of the X-T2's contrast detection autofocus (CDAF): XF16–55mmF2.8 R LM WR; XF50–140mmF2.8 R LM OIS WR; XF90mmF2 R LM WR; XF35mmF2 R WR, XF100–400mmF4.5–5.6 R LM OIS WR, and the XF23mmF2 R WR.

In addition to native X-mount lenses, you can also attach a host of current and older lenses from other manufacturers to the X-T2 with the use of a suitable adapter. Remember that adapted lenses will always operate either wide open or at the set working aperture. Autofocus, program AE, and shutter priority AE will not be available, either.

> X-mount compatible **Samyang lenses** are just like adapted lenses!   **TIP 12**

Manual focus lenses from Samyang (Rokinon) and similar brands aren't native X-mount lenses. They simply come with a compatible mechanical mount so you don't have to buy an additional adapter. These lenses behave like other adapted third-party lenses: they don't communicate with the camera (there's no data transmission because there aren't any electronic contacts), there's no autofocus, the live view [08] operates with the currently set working aperture, and you can only use modes **A** and **M**.

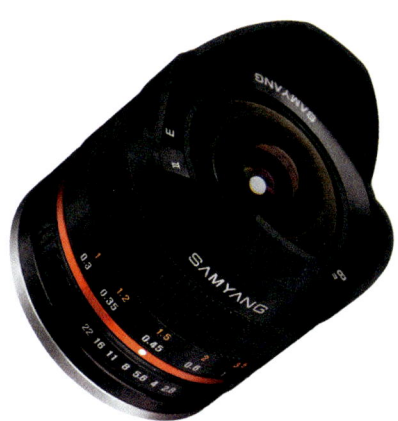

Fig. 12:
The affordable **Samyang 8mmF2.8 Fisheye II** manual focus lens for Fujifilm X-mount is a popular choice to record images with extreme angles.

| TIP 13 | Zeiss Touit lenses |

Even though Touit lenses with native X-mount compatibility offer great image quality and work like Fujinon XF lenses, Zeiss tends to be hesitant to support new camera features with lens firmware updates. It took Zeiss about half a year longer than Fuji to offer PDAF support, and there is still no LMO support. There's also no indication that Zeiss wants to continue with the Touit line of lenses.

| TIP 14 | Decoding XF18–135mmF3.5–5.6 R LM OIS WR |

This tip is of the "what you always wanted to know but never dared to ask" variety:

- **XF:** "X" means X-mount or X-series; "F" means Fine, for Fuji's premium line of lenses. There's also the smaller, more affordable XC line ("C" stands for Compact or Casual).

- **18–135mm:** This is the focal length range of the zoom lens. To translate the numbers to their full-frame equivalents, you have to multiply them by the APS-C crop factor [09] of 1.5. Hence, the field-of-view (FOV) of an 18–135mm zoom on your X-T2 is identical to the FOV of a 27–202mm zoom lens on a full-frame camera.

- **F3.5–5.6:** This range describes the maximum aperture opening at the low and high end of the focal-length range. In this case, the lens offers a maximum aperture of f/3.5 at 18mm and f/5.6 at 135mm.

- **R:** This stands for Ring and simply means that the lens features an aperture ring. This is a standard feature of all Fujinon XF lenses, with the exception of the XF27mmF2.8 pancake lens. XC zooms don't offer an aperture ring, either. With those lenses, the aperture setting is controlled with the command dial when you are using exposure modes **A** or **M**.

- **LM:** This stands for Linear Motor, which ensures quick and silent autofocus operation.

- **OIS:** This is the Optical Image Stabilizer [10]. This feature allows you to perform handheld shots at up to five stops slower of a shutter speed than you would usually need to eliminate camera shake. For example, in situations that would normally require a shutter speed of 1/80s to ensure a clear image, you could shoot with 1/4s and still get usable results. It's important to remember that motion blur often plays a role at slower shutter speeds since many subjects tend to move. Obviously the OIS cannot reduce motion blur [11]—only blurring that occurs due to camera shake (i.e., the shaky hands of the photographer).

- **WR** denotes weather resistant lenses. These lenses are a great fit for your weather resistant X-T2.

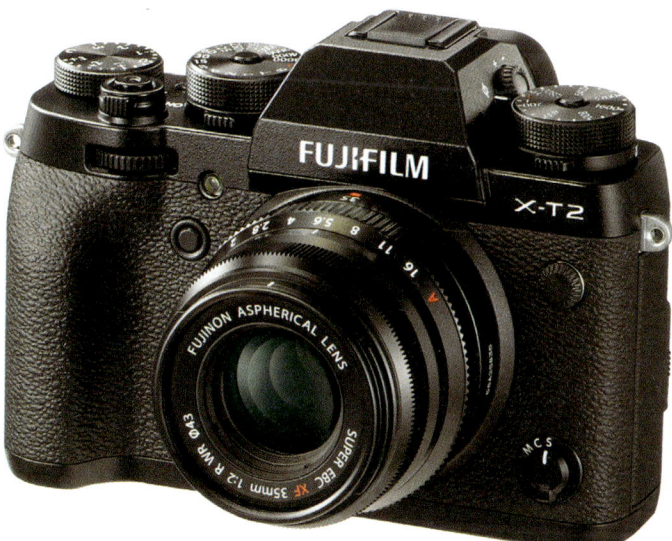

Fig. 13: The **XF35mmF2 R WR** is Fujifilm's best-selling prime lens for the X-series. It's weather resistant, and its lean design doesn't obscure the optical viewfinder of the X-Pro1 and X-Pro2.

| TIP 15 | The **optical image stabilizer (OIS)** has its quirks! |

With the exception of the XF16–55mmF2.8 R LM WR zoom, all XF and XC zoom lenses feature built-in optical image stabilization (OIS). Switch on the OIS to prevent camera shake and blurry images in situations that require you to take handheld shots at a slower-than-usual shutter speed. XF lenses offer a dedicated OIS on/off switch on the lens barrel. The OIS in XC lenses is controlled through a camera menu.

For handheld shots, an old rule of thumb recommends using shutter speeds that are at least as fast as the reciprocal of the full-frame-equivalent focal length that is in use. For example, with a 50mm lens and an APS-C crop factor of 1.5, the minimum safe shutter speed for handheld camera use would be $[1/(50 \times 1.5)]s = 1/75s$. In other words, when you are shooting handheld with a 50mm lens and don't want shaky images, you should use shutter speeds at least as fast as 1/75s. Or you can use the OIS to add a few more stops.

Of course, rules of thumb don't apply to everybody. Some users have quite steady hands and some are rather shaky. The settings and equipment that work for me may not work for you. However, the OIS will always give you a few extra stops of shutter-speed headroom.

In SHOOTING SETTING > IS MODE, you can choose between two basic OIS modes:

- **OIS mode 1** (CONTINUOUS) is the default setting. It's always stabilizing the image, even when you are just looking through the viewfinder before you press the shutter button.

- **OIS mode 2** (SHOOTING ONLY) only engages when you fully depress the shutter button to take an image.

Please note that the OIS can also *introduce* camera shake, especially at fast shutter speeds. This adverse effect is more likely to occur in OIS mode 1 than in mode 2. However, OIS mode 1 is more effective when used at very slow shutter speeds, such as 1/15s, 1/8s, or even 1/4s.

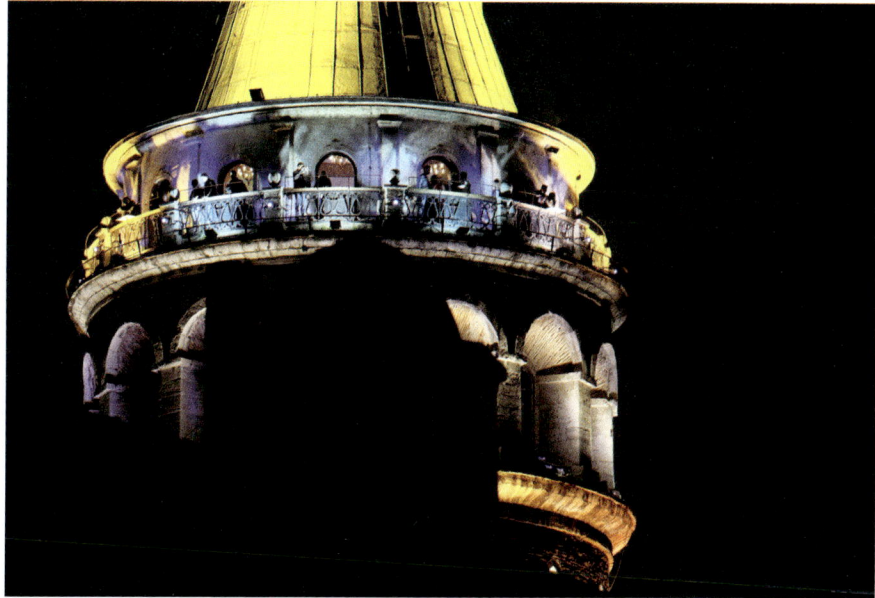

Fig. 14: The **optical image stabilizer** of the XF50–140mm in action: Thanks to a slow shutter speed of 1/6s, I could still use ISO 800 for this night shot. Even at a full-frame equivalent of 210mm, the OIS was able to successfully compensate for any camera shake caused by my hands.

These are my recommendations for using the OIS:

■ Only use (switch on) the OIS when necessary. When you are using fast shutter speeds that don't require image stabilization, you can safely turn the OIS off to eliminate it as a potential interference.

■ I prefer to use the OIS in mode 2 ("shooting only"). Mode 1 is useful at very slow shutter speeds and when you are using very long focal lengths because the camera will also stabilize the live view image, making it easier to compose and focus a shot.

■ Turn off the OIS when you are working from a sturdy tripod or with shutter speeds that are slower than a second.
You should also switch it off for panning [12] shots.

By the way, the OIS emits a soft humming sound, even when
the function is turned off. Don't worry about the noise.

TIP 16	The XF23mmF1.4 R, XF16mmF1.4 R WR, and XF14mmF2.8 R are different beasts!

Unlike standard X-mount lenses, the wide-angle primes
XF14mmF2.8 R, XF16mmF1.4 R WR, and **XF23mmF1.4 R**
feature a more traditional manual focus ring with a clutch
mechanism:

■ Pull the focus ring towards the camera to set the lens to
manual focus.

■ Push the focus ring away from the camera to set the lens
to autofocus.

■ Alternatively, you can use the traditional focus selector switch at the front of the camera to set the X-T2 to
manual focus mode. In this case, the lens remains in
autofocus mode, and you can only use the AF-L button
(Instant AF) to change the focus. This also means that you
cannot manually adjust your focus after focusing with
Instant AF.

■ You cannot use Instant AF (AF-L button) to focus when
the focus ring of the lens is set to manual focus. In this
case, you can only use the manual focus ring to change
or adjust the focus.

■ The analog depth-of-field (DOF) markers on the lens
barrel correspond with the X-T2's electronic film format-
based scale and are less conservative (and in my opinion
less useful) than the camera's pixel-based scale. This is
because the pixel-based scale is using a much smaller
circle of confusion [13] in order to display DOF ranges

with pixel-sharp results at 100% magnification, whereas the engraved scale on the lens uses a value that's based on looking at typically sized prints from a typical distance with typical eyesight. Some photographers regard the engraved scale (which equals the electronic film format-based scale) as more practical. Personally, I prefer the pixel-based scale. In any case, the actual difference between the two scales is about 3.5 aperture stops. To switch between the film format-based and the pixel-based electronic DOF displays, select AF/MF SETTING > DEPTH-OF-FIELD SCALE and then select either PIXEL BASIS or FILM FORMAT BASIS.

- It's not possible to reverse the focusing direction of the manual focus ring with the 14mm, 16mm, or 23mm lenses.

- If you set your X-T2 to AF+MF mode (AF/MF SETTING > AF+MF > ON), you can only use this feature when the lens clutch is set to MF and the camera to AF-S. In this configuration, you can autofocus by half-pressing the shutter button, and then manually adjusting the focus with the focus ring (while keeping the shutter button half-pressed).

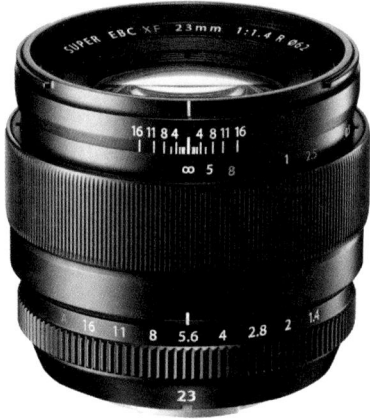

Fig. 15: Fujinon XF23mmF1.4 R with engraved distance and DOF markers. It's a nice retro touch, but you lose some state-of-the-art digital functionality.

| TIP 17 | Use the **Lens Modulation Optimizer** (LMO)! |

The X-T2 supports the Lens Modulation Optimizer or LMO. This feature premiered in the X100S and X20 fixed-lens cameras, and it counteracts common optical phenomena (like diffraction [14] and corner softness) when the camera converts the RAW data into JPEG images. To make it work, the firmware in the attached lens sends the LMO correction data to the camera.

- Neither Fujinon XC lenses nor Zeiss Touit lenses support the LMO.

If your lens supports the LMO (all Fujinon XF lenses do), you should enable the function by selecting LENS MODULATION OPTIMIZER > ON in the IMAGE QUALITY SETTING menu.

You can also use the built-in RAW converter of your X-T2 (PLAYBACK MENU > RAW CONVERSION) to enable or disable the LMO for a specific image. With this method, it's easy to create and compare versions of a shot with and without LMO enhancements.

In its current incarnation, the LMO takes care of the following two optical effects:

- **Diffraction softness:** This effect increasingly occurs when the lens is stopped down beyond a certain point. APS-C cameras like the X-T2 typically exhibit diffraction at apertures of 10 and smaller. While stopping down increases the overall depth of field (DOF), it also reduces the maximum resolution of the lens/camera combination. The LMO counteracts this effect and reconstructs some of the lost detail.

- **Corner softness:** Even the best lenses aren't as sharp in the corners as they are in the center. The LMO in the X-T2 is able to digitally compensate for that loss of quality.

LMO corrections are based on complex deconvolution [15] algorithms. Currently, this is only supported in-camera with the built-in RAW converter. External converters such as Lightroom, Adobe Camera Raw, Capture One Pro, Silkypix, Iridient Developer, Photo Ninja, and AccuRaw can't process LMO data. This means that LMO corrections are only visible in JPEGs that are generated in the camera.

Things you should know about **digital lens corrections:**	TIP 18

Most modern lenses achieve their optimal image quality through a combination of optical and digital corrections. Corrections are mostly applied to the three following phenomena:

- **Vignetting:** This effect results in a loss of brightness from center to corner. Vignetting [16] is more pronounced at large (open) apertures.

- **Distortion:** There are pincushion- and barrel-type distortions [17], both of which make straight lines seem curved. Premium primes like the XF14mm, XF23mm, XF35mmF1.4, XF56mm, and XF90mm are fully optically corrected for distortion. Others (such as the Zeiss Touit range, compact pancake lenses, the XF35mmF2, or zoom lenses) require a combination of optical and digital distortion correction.

- **Chromatic aberration:** Chromatic aberration [18] results in color fringing. This effect can be corrected (or mitigated) with apochromatic lenses, or digitally corrected during RAW conversion.

Some camera makers rely on dedicated correction profiles that have to be provided by each RAW converter maker. Fujifilm isn't one of these companies: all current Fujifilm cameras store digital corrections as metadata in the RAW file. RAW converters can access this lens-specific metadata and use it to apply appropriate corrections. This way, the built-in RAW converter and external software, such as Lightroom, Silkypix, Iridient Developer, or Capture One, can use the metadata in the RAW file to correct or mitigate vignetting, distortion, and chromatic aberration.

A major benefit of this method is that many RAW converters automatically support new lenses since Fujifilm delivers the correction data via the RAW metadata. However, there's also a drawback: some RAW converters (such as Lightroom, Adobe Camera Raw, and Silkypix) don't give you the option to switch off metadata-based digital lens corrections, even if you're convinced they aren't necessary. Since digital distortion correction always results in some loss of image sharpness and detail due to the required stretching and interpolation, this can be a headache for some users. Obviously, not all subjects or images require the same amount of digital correction (it can also be a simple matter of taste), so full user control over the application of digital lens corrections is a very nice feature.

Luckily, software like Iridient Developer and Capture One offer control over how much digital metadata distortion (or vignetting) correction should be applied. Other programs (like Photo Ninja, Raw Photo Processor/RPP, and AccuRaw) simply ignore lens correction metadata. With such programs, all corrections have to be applied either manually or by using a dedicated profile.

TIP 19	Use the included **lens hood!**

With the single exception of the XF27mmF2.8 pancake lens, all Fujifilm XF and XC lenses come with a fitted lens hood, which should be used whenever possible. Apart from its optical benefits, the hood protects the lens and the front glass element from damage.

Lens hoods can pose problems, too: they make the lens appear bigger than it actually is, and they can shade the camera flash or the autofocus assist light. They also use up extra space in your bag, although most hoods can be reverse-mounted on the lens for transport purposes.

When you shoot with a small shoe-mounted flash, or when you depend on using the AF assist lamp, it's best to remove the lens hood.

Lens protection filters—yes or no?	TIP 20

Digital cameras like the X-T2 don't require the UV or skylight filters that used to be very popular in the days of analog film photography. This means that a permanently affixed filter has no optical purpose, and only serves as protective glass. This additional glass can have a negative effect on image quality, especially at night or when you shoot against a bright light source. Filters increase the chance of ghosting, unwanted reflections, or a loss of contrast.

This is why I recommend using protective glass only in situations that actually require this additional protective layer. In most situations, the lens hood should provide suf-ficient protection. If you still decide to use a filter, make sure to choose a high-quality product. Fujifilm offers suitable protective filters that feature the same Super EBC coating used on all of their XF/XC lenses. Be prepared to pay a pre-mium, though.

39mm filters can be tricky!	TIP 21

The **XF60mmF2.4 R** and **XF27mmF2.8** lenses require filters with a 39mm thread. It's important that those filters are designed to allow the inner lens barrel to freely retract into the outer barrel while the filter is attached. If this isn't possible (for example, because a thin step-up ring is directly attached to the lens or because the filter's overall diameter is too large), the lens can be damaged when the filter or step-up ring collides with the outer barrel of the lens.

A typical indicator for this and other mechanical lens problems is a message alerting you that the camera needs to be switched off and on again. A possible solution is putting a spacer (a suitable 39mm filter, for example) between the lens and the step-up ring. You should remove the glass from the spacer, so any cheap/old/unused 39mm filter will do the job as long as it fits and doesn't interfere with the outer lens barrel when the inner barrel is retracting.

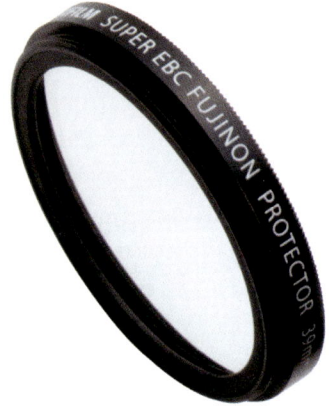

Fig. 16: A **39mm protection filter** by Fujifilm. A filter like this can also be used as a spacer between the lens (XF60mm or XF27mm) and a step-up ring.

1.3 THE BASICS (3): USEFUL ACCESSORIES

There's a rich selection of accessories for your X-T2. Whether or not you believe such add-ons are useful, I'll cover a few select items that can, in my opinion and experience, improve the functionality of your camera.

Optional handgrips	TIP 22

An optional handgrip can improve the ergonomics of the X-T2 when you are using large, heavy lenses or if you have large hands.

The **MHG-XT2** provides full access to the battery compartment, and is compatible with Arca-Swiss-type tripod heads, so you don't need a dedicated quick release plate. The handgrip *is* the quick release plate.

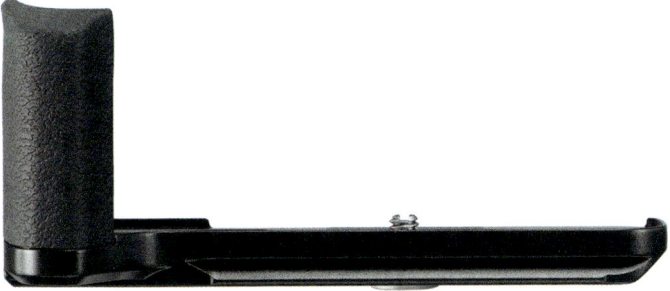

Fig. 17: The optional **handgrip MHG-XT2** provides direct access to the battery compartment and can be mounted on an Arca-Swiss-type tripod head.

The **Vertical Power Booster Grip** is another useful option to enhance both the ergonomics and the performance of your X-T2. The grip can fit two batteries to boost the maximum number of shots per charge to approximately 1,000.

For improved vertical shooting, the grip mirrors the camera body's shutter release button, Q button, focus stick, both command dials, the AE-L/AF-L buttons, and one Fn button. The tripod-mounting socket is in line with the camera's optical axis, and the grip is resistant to dust and water. It offers its own battery-charging functionality and is capable of fully charging two batteries in two hours with the included power supply.

The Vertical Power Booster Grip also features a dedicated Boost mode switch that improves AF speed and the EVF refresh rate. When fitted with the grip, the camera uses multiple batteries simultaneously to improve its performance on aspects such as 4K video recording, continuous shooting, shooting interval, shutter release time lag, and blackout time.

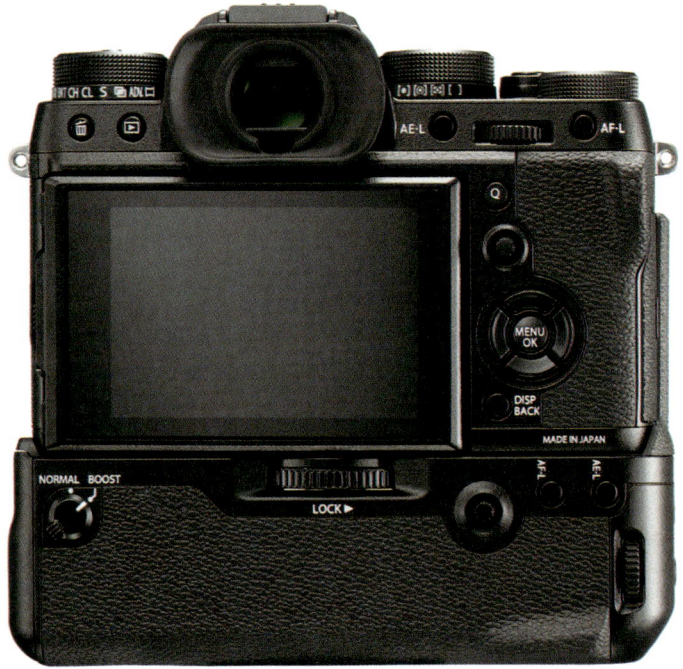

Fig. 18: The **Vertical Power Booster Grip** is a useful companion for the X-T2. Personally, I almost never take it off. It enhances the camera's usability with large and heavy lenses, offers improved ergonomics for vertical shooting, and features a headphone output for videographers. Its most important features are the addition of up to two batteries and its performance-boosting capabilities. With a total of three batteries in the camera body and the grip, users can spend a day of intense shooting without changing or charging batteries.

| Off-camera TTL flash with a Canon OC-E3 TTL extension cord | TIP 23 |

Basically, the X-T2 can be combined with most third-party flashes, as long as the flash output is controlled manually. However, Fuji's automated TTL flash exposure (called Super Intelligent Flash in a grossly exaggerated fashion) currently only works with Fujifilm compatible TTL flash units like the **EF-20, EF-X20,** and **EF-42,** or the **Nissin i40**. In late 2016, Fujifilm also added the professional **EF-X500** flash unit to the lineup. The EF-X500 allows wireless TTL and FP high-speed-sync (HSS).

TTL is an abbreviation for "Through The Lens," which means that the camera determines the appropriate flash output by measuring a scene through the lens with a weak pre-flash. In order to work in TTL mode, TTL flash units have to be connected with the camera's hot shoe, and strangely enough, there's still no Fujifilm-branded TTL extension cable on the market that allows you to use a TTL flash off-camera. A simple solution is using a **Canon OC-E3** extension cable, which is pin-compatible with Fuji's flash contacts. With such a cable (or a compatible third-party product), it is possible to use an EF-20, EF-X20, EF-42, EF-X500, or another Fuji TTL compatible flash off-camera in TTL mode. Please note that Canon OC-E3 cables are only compatible with Fuji's TTL flash *connectors,* not with Fuji's TTL flash *protocol.* This means that it isn't possible to use Canon TTL flash devices with an X-T2 in TTL mode.

Fujifilm's compact (and retro-styled) EF-X20 flash features an optical slave mode and can be wirelessly triggered by another flash unit. However, this is no automated TTL mode, so the output of the EF-X20 has to be manually controlled while in slave mode.

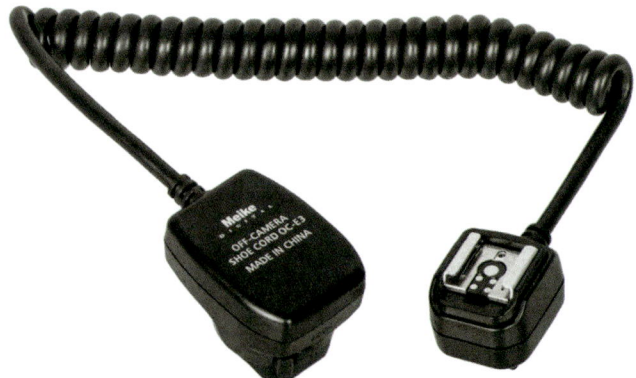

Fig. 19: A **Canon-compatible TTL extension cord** works with the X-T2. However, since the extra power line for Fuji's tiny EF-X8 flash unit isn't looped through, this flash can only be used directly on the camera's hot-show mount.

TIP 24	Issues regarding **Canon TTL flash devices**

Canon-compatible flash devices (e.g., flash units or radio transmitters) can lead to an overload of the X-Pro2's processor and result in overheating (you'll see the related overheating warnings if this happens), so there's reason to believe that the X-T2 may also be affected. It's caused by incompatible Canon/Fuji TTL flash protocols that are routed through compatible flash contacts, as described in the previous tip.

This problem can even occur when you are using your Canon-compatible flash gear in full manual mode without any expectation of TTL exposure control. You might want a simple trigger signal, but what you get are colliding protocols with adverse side effects.

Should you encounter these problems with your gear, you have three basic choices:

- Stop using your Canon-compatible TTL flash or transmitter and replace it with simpler devices that only use a central trigger contact.

■ Tape the TTL contacts of your flash devices, leaving only the central trigger contact. This ensures that the only electric connection between the camera and the flash or transmitter is the flash trigger contact.

■ Use an adapter that isolates the flash sync signal and blocks all other hot-shoe pin connections to your flash device. This is like taping TTL pins, just more convenient. Suitable adapters are available for only a few dollars.

Please note that flawless flash operation is only guaranteed when you use devices that explicitly support the Fujifilm X flash system and protocol. Alternatively, you can also use simple, manual flash devices and transmitters that only use the camera's central trigger contact. Other flash devices (that were originally made for other camera brands and systems) may also work in full manual mode, but there's no guarantee for it. Proceed at your own risk.

Remote shutter release: three options for the X T2	TIP 25

Now and then you may encounter situations that require you to remotely release the shutter without vibration. A quick-and-dirty method is using the camera's self-timer with a delay of either two or ten seconds, although a better way is using a remote shutter release. Your X-T2 features three different ports to connect remote shutter releases:

■ A **mechanical thread** in the shutter button allows you to connect a traditional cable release.

■ There's an **RR-90 port** (Micro-USB port) that is compatible with a variety of electronic remote controls.

■ You can connect electronic remote shutter releases to the camera's **microphone port** (a 2.5mm input).

Electronic shutter releases are available in tethered and wireless versions. Wireless options always consist of a transmitter and a receiver. The transmitter sends a trigger signal that is picked up by the receiver, which triggers the camera with an electronic cable that's connected to the RR-90 or remote port.

Fujifilm offers a simple RR-90-compatible shutter release cable, but there are more sophisticated (both tethered and wireless) solutions from third parties, such as programmable intervalometers.

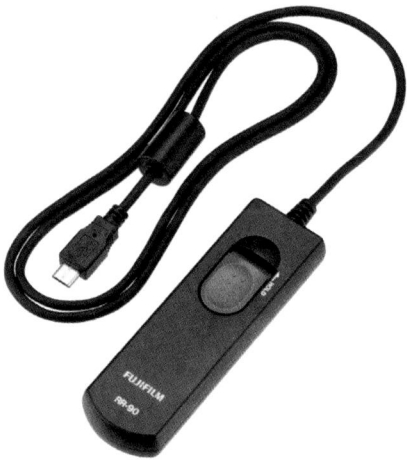

Fig. 20: Fujifilm's RR-90 is a simple and reliable remote for your X-T2.

If you already own an older RR-80-type shutter release (which was the standard for the X-E1), you can buy a third-party adapter cable that lets you use RR-80 remote shutter releases with RR-90 cameras. Please note that a simple USB adapter doesn't work; you have to ask for a dedicated RR-80 to RR-90 adapter.

The microphone port of the X-T2 is compatible with a widely used Canon remote shutter release standard. Among others, it is compatible to the following camera models: Canon EOS Digital Rebel, Canon EOS 1000D, Canon EOS 100D, Canon EOS 1100D, Canon EOS 300D, Canon EOS 350D, Canon EOS 400D, Canon EOS 450D, Canon EOS 500D,

Canon EOS 550D, Canon EOS 600D, Canon EOS 60D, Canon EOS 60Da, Canon EOS 650D, Canon EOS 700D, Canon EOS Kiss Digital, Canon EOS Kiss F, Canon EOS Kiss Digital N, Canon EOS Kiss X2, Canon EOS Kiss X3, Canon EOS Kiss X4, Canon EOS Kiss X5, Canon EOS Kiss X50, Canon EOS Kiss X6i, Canon PowerShot G1 X, Canon PowerShot G10, Canon PowerShot G11, Canon PowerShot G12, Canon PowerShot G15, Canon PowerShot SX50 HS, Canon EOS Rebel SL1, Canon EOS Rebel T1i, Canon EOS Rebel 70 T2i, Canon EOS Rebel T3, Canon EOS Rebel T3i, Canon EOS Rebel T4i, Canon EOS Rebel XS, Canon EOS Rebel XSi, Canon EOS Rebel XT, Canon EOS Rebel XTi, Canon EOS Rebel T5i, Contax 645, Contax N, Contax N Digital, Contax N1, Contax NX, Hasselblad H1, Hasselblad H3D, Hasselblad H4D-200MS, Hasselblad H4D-31, Hasselblad H4D-40, Hasselblad H4D-50, Hasselblad H4D-50MS, Hasselblad H4D-60, Pentax 645D, Pentax *ist D, Pentax *ist DL, Pentax *ist DL2, Pentax *ist DS, Pentax *ist DS2, Pentax K-30, Pentax K-5, Pentax K-7, Pentax K-m, Pentax K10 Grand Prix, Pentax K100D, Pentax K100D Super, Pentax K10D, Pentax K110D, Pentax K200D, Pentax K20D, Pentax MZ-6, Pentax MZ-L, Pentax ZX-L, Samsung GX-1L, Samsung GX-1S, Samsung GX-20, Samsung NX10, Samsung NX100, Samsung NX11, Samsung NX5, Sigma SD1, Sigma SD1 Merrill, and Sigma SD15.

This list isn't complete, but it's a pretty good start. Remote shutter releases that are compatible with any of these listed cameras should also work with the your X-T2.

Triggertrap Mobile is a smart and flexible way to trigger cameras with a smartphone (Android or iOS). In order to make it work with an X-T2, you need a dongle and an adapter cable. You can read more about this on Triggertrap's official website [19].

Of course, you can also remotely control the camera using its built-in Wi-fi function and the free Fujifilm Camera Remote app [20] for iOS or Android devices.

2. USING THE FUJIFILM X-T2

2.1 READY, SET, GO!

New users often ask about how to achieve the perfect settings for their camera. Short answer: there are no perfect settings. If they existed, Fuji could have saved us the trouble of navigating the menu options and simply implemented those ideal settings as the factory default.

Obviously, this short answer isn't satisfactory to readers of this book, so here's a more thorough one:

- Years of practical experience with digital Fujifilm cameras have lead me to suggest a set of recommended basic settings that are meant to provide good overall performance and as much flexibility as possible.

- Many settings (such as film simulation modes, color saturation, contrast, sharpness, noise reduction, film grain effect, etc.) belong in the "JPEG settings" category. They don't affect the RAW files; only the out-of-camera JPEGs that are generated during RAW conversion. These settings aren't global or camera-specific—they are image-specific and each image should be adjusted individually.

- In addition to the recommended standard settings, there are a number of shortcuts and key combinations that can make choosing the optimal camera settings for any situation much easier.

TIP 26	**Recommended settings** for your X-T2

There is no perfect set of basic camera settings that could suit all users in all situations. However, the following settings will allow you to use the X-T2 in a flexible manner with good overall performance:

- **Auto-ISO** is a convenient option with three presets that can be selected by setting the ISO dial to "A" and selecting one of three Auto-ISO choices (AUTO1–3) with SHOOT-ING SETTING > ISO AUTO SETTING. The corresponding Auto-ISO fine-tuning is available for each Auto-ISO preset by pressing the right selector button. There, you can adjust DEFAULT SENSITIVITY (I suggest 200), MAX. SENSITIVITY (I suggest 12800) and MIN. SHUTTER SPEED. Don't worry: even at the upper limit of ISO 12800, images made with the X-Trans sensor are quite good. When you are using Auto-ISO, you should pick a suitable minimum shutter speed with MIN. SHUTTER SPEED. A popular setting for the minimum shutter speed is 1/60s, but you can change this parameter to anything between 1/4s and 1/500s. Using a stabilized (OIS) lens, speeds slower than 1/60s are definitely a realistic option for this camera. With fast-moving objects, faster speeds are recommended to avoid unwanted motion blur. My personal minimum shutter speed settings for AUTO1, AUTO2, and AUTO3 are 1/60s (landscape), 1/200s (portraits), and 1/500s (action).

- Always select **FINE+RAW** under IMAGE QUALITY SET-TING > IMAGE QUALITY or in the Quick menu. This will get you high-resolution out-of-camera JPEGs (digital prints) *and* flexible RAW files (digital negatives). Using the RAW files, you can create a variety of diverse JPEGs with different looks and settings using the camera's built-in RAW converter (PLAYBACK MENU > RAW CON-VERSION). Specifically, you can adjust JPEG parameters such as white balance, film simulations, contrast, bright-ness, noise reduction, and color saturation. This enables you to create different versions of a shot from a single RAW file; for example, you can make both color and black-and-white versions of the same image, including different contrast settings. You don't have to worry about choosing the perfect JPEG settings prior to taking a shot because you can always change and optimize those settings afterward in the camera's internal RAW converter.

- As a typical standard setting, most photographers use **single shot drive** (select S on the DRIVE dial) and **single shot autofocus** (AF-S; select S with the focus selector at the front of the camera).

- The most flexible and accurate AF-S setting is **Single Point AF** (AF/MF SETTING > AF MODE > SINGLE POINT). This mode allows you to select the area of the image where the camera should be focused. To accomplish this, use either the focus stick or select AF/MF SETTING > FOCUS AREA, then use the selector keys (arrow keys) or the focus stick to pick one of the 91 or 325 available AF frames. There, you can change the size of the selected AF frame by turning any of the command dials. *Pressing* (not turning) the rear command dial resets the frame to its default size. Pressing the DISP/BACK button (or the focus stick) selects the central (default) AF frame. Press OK or half-press the shutter button to confirm your selection. The camera will use this frame in AF-S and AF-C modes as its focus area as soon as you press or half-press the shutter button.

- Unlike most DSLR cameras, the X-T2 uses a **hybrid autofocus system**: a blend of contrast detection autofocus (CDAF) and phase detection autofocus (PDAF). The main burden still rests on the CDAF, which covers all AF frames (most of the sensor area). The PDAF is only covered by the central AF frames (about 40% of the sensor area). It's faster, but only works in sufficiently good light. Both AF methods work most precisely with a small AF frame, but work faster and more reliably with a large AF frame. This leads to an obvious conflict of interest. My basic AF frame size rule is: always select an AF frame that is as large as possible, but as small as necessary.

- Set your X-T2 to maximum performance by selecting SET UP > POWER MANAGEMENT > PERFORMANCE > BOOST. This option is *not* enabled by default, so you have to manually select it. Only **Boost mode** unleashes the full potential of the camera, offering the fastest available live view readout and best autofocus performance. This mode also uses up more energy, so make sure to always carry one or two fully charged replacement batteries.

- To further improve AF performance, you can select AF/MF SETTING > PRE-AF > ON. **Pre-AF** makes the camera focus on whatever is covered by the currently selected AF frame or zone, even when the shutter button is *not* pressed or half-pressed. This can save valuable split seconds when you actually take a shot, but it also means that the camera is using up more energy. Worse, in this mode the lens is always focusing on something, so it may make distracting noises. For these reasons, I *don't* recommend using Pre-AF as your default setting. Only use it under special circumstances.

- Set AF/MF SETTING > RELEASE/FOCUS PRIORITY to FOCUS for both AF-S and AF-C. **Focus Priority** makes sure that the camera records a picture only when the autofocus thinks that it has locked onto a target. In RELEASE mode, the X-T2 will take the shot even if the autofocus couldn't find a lock. Please note that if you are using AF+MF mode, AF-S will always operate with release priority. By the way: my recommended default setting for AF/MF SETTING > AF+MF is ON.

- If you want to quickly take a series of single shots, I recommend selecting SET UP > SCREEN SET-UP > IMAGE DISP. > OFF in order to not interrupt your flow. However, I *normally* set **Image Display** to 0.5 SEC, because I like to see a quick preview of the final image that represents the camera's dynamic range (DR) settings. To cancel an ongoing image preview and continue shooting, simply half-press the shutter button.

■ By pressing the DISP/BACK button, you can choose between different live view display modes: For the LCD, you can pick live views with or without an information overlay, and an INFO display mode that displays your current camera and exposure settings. For the EVF, you have a choice of two live view image sizes, both with information overlays. In manual focus (MF) mode, there is an additional split screen option for both the LCD and EVF, also with information overlays. The overlay options offer essential tools like the electronic level, the live histogram, or the electronic distance and DOF scale. To choose which elements you want displayed, select SET UP > SCREEN SET-UP > DISP. CUSTOM SETTNG, then pick the desired elements from the list. Make sure to enable the live histogram! Personally, I select *all* available options in this menu. Please note that you can select the display mode *independently* for the viewfinder (EVF) and the LCD. Pressing the DISP/BACK button only affects the currently active view (either the viewfinder or the rear LCD). In order to change the display mode of the viewfinder, it must be active when you press the DISP/BACK button—this means you must be looking through the viewfinder while the eye sensor is active.

■ Use the VIEW MODE button to activate the **eye sensor,** which will allow the camera to automatically switch between the viewfinder (EVF) and the LCD depending on which view is in use. There's also an alternative mode called EVF ONLY + EYE SENSOR, which is an energy-saving mode. This mode can make it more difficult to operate the camera, because the LCD won't be available for changing menus while in shooting mode.

■ For **exposure metering,** I recommend using MULTI metering as your default mode. Intelligent matrix metering usually delivers results that don't require a massive amount of exposure correction. You can select the metering mode with the metering dial, which is located under the shutter speed dial.

■ Set IMAGE QUALITY SETTING > WHITE BALANCE > AUTO to let the camera set the correct **white balance** for a scene. Since you are shooting FINE+RAW, you can always adjust the white balance later, either with the camera's built-in RAW converter or with external RAW conversion software such as Adobe Lightroom. That said, AUTO will deliver very good results in most scenarios.

■ If you want to keep things (too) simple, you can select IMAGE QUALITY SETTING > DYNAMIC RANGE > AUTO as your default setting. This enables the X-T2 to automatically determine whether or not a scene requires an extra stop of **dynamic range** (DR). In this mode, the camera either shoots the scene in DR100% (standard mode) or in DR200% (with an extra stop of dynamic range in the highlights). Please note that DR400% (for *two* extra stops of dynamic range in the highlights) is only available by manual selection, not in DR AUTO mode. Extending the dynamic range maintains the texture in the bright areas of your shot (such as white clouds on a sunny day) and prevents them from appearing blown out. Personally, I want to be in control of my dynamic range setting, so I always set DR manually with a default of DR100%.

■ To use **adapted lenses** with your X-T2, you need either Fujifilm's Leica M adapter or a suitable third-party adapter. In order to make third-party adapters work, you have to select SET UP > BUTTON/DIAL SETTING > SHOOT WITHOUT LENS > ON. This is necessary because adapted lenses (and third-party lens adapters) do not feature electronic X-mount contacts, so the lens will not register as being connected to the camera. When you are working with an adapted lens, you should also enter its focal length in SHOOTING SETTING > MOUNT ADAPTOR SETTING. This ensures that the EXIF [21] data will show the proper focal length.

■ Do you sometimes shoot with very slow shutter speeds lasting several seconds? In this case, I recommend setting IMAGE QUALITY SETTING > LONG EXPOSURE NR > ON to improve the quality of your results. In this mode, the X-T2 performs a so-called dark-frame subtraction [22] to reduce noise and eliminate hot pixels. With this process, the total exposure time is doubled because the camera is taking the shot twice: once normally and once with a closed shutter curtain. The second shot is then subtracted from the first to improve the overall result.

■ I recommend *not* using the AUTO setting for the **brightness control for the EVF** because it tends to show an overly bright live view image in bright sunlight and a very subdued image when it's dark. Instead, I set SET UP > SCREEN SET-UP > EVF BRIGHTNESS > MANUAL with a setting of 0. I use the same setting for the rear LCD.

■ For the purpose of this book, we assume that SHUTTER AF and SHUTTER AE (in the SET UP > BUTTON DIAL SETTING menu) are both set to ON, which is also the X-T2's factory default setting. This ensures that autofocus and exposure (including the working aperture) are locked when you half-press the shutter button, so the camera is primed for the least possible shutter lag once you continue to fully press the shutter button.

■ I select SET UP > BUTTON DIAL SETTING > COMMAND DIAL SETTING > S.S. F to ensure that the X-T2 stays in line with other X-series cameras that use the front command dial to adjust the shutter speed, and the rear command dial to adjust the aperture (when a lens without an aperture ring is used). All related recommendations in this book are based on this setting.

Avoiding the camera menus: **practical shortcuts** for your X-T2 | **TIP 27**

Navigating nested camera menus can be cumbersome. That's why the X-T2 offers the Quick menu (Q button) and user-configurable Fn keys that can provide direct access to important and frequently used camera functions and settings.

The X-T2 also offers seven custom user settings (C1 through C7) that can hold groups of frequently used camera settings. You can select one of these groups (or profiles) via the Quick menu or an appropriately configured Fn key. C1 through C7 aren't camera *modes;* they are memory locations. Each one conveniently stores a configured profile. Use these as shortcuts to immediately change your current camera settings to another predefined set of options.

Finally, the X-T2 offers a so-called MY MENU, where you can arrange frequently used menu items on configurable menu pages for quick and easy access.

Speaking of shortcuts—there are plenty, and most of them are available at your fingertips:

■ Pull up the Quick menu, then press and hold the Q button again for a few seconds to directly open the configuration menu for your custom user settings (C1 to C7).

■ Press and hold the Q button while the Quick menu is *not* open to directly access the Quick menu configuration page. In this mode, you can customize the Quick menu to meet your personal requirements. You can assign one of more than two dozen different settings to any of the 16 available Quick menu elements. If you don't need 16 shortcuts, you can even select NONE to reduce the size of the Quick menu and make it easier to navigate.

■ Press and hold the MENU/OK button to lock the selector keys and the Q button. Press and hold the MENU/OK button again to remove the key lock.

- To see where the Fn buttons are located and what's assigned to each of them, simply press and hold the DISP/BACK button. In this menu, you can also reassign all Fn buttons.

- To confirm a new menu selection in shooting mode, you can either press the MENU/OK button or half-press the shutter button.

- Half-press the shutter button to switch from playback mode to shooting mode.

- Half-press the shutter button during an ongoing image preview (SET UP > SCREEN SET-UP > IMAGE DISP.) to immediately cancel the preview.

- Half-press the shutter button for a few seconds to wake-up the camera from sleep mode.

- In AF-S shooting mode (with Single Point AF) or MF mode, press the rear command dial to zoom into the currently active AF frame. When zoomed-in, you can choose between two magnification levels by turning the command dial.

- Press and hold the rear command dial in MF mode to cycle between the different manual focus assist modes: standard, focus peaking, and digital split image.

- You can move the selected AF frame or zone around with the four selector (arrow) keys. Press the DISP/BACK button to reset the position of the AF frame or AF zone to the center. You can change the size of the selected AF frame or zone by turning one of the command dials. To reset the size of the AF frame or zone to default, press one of the command dials.

- Press and hold the focus stick in shooting mode to access the focus stick options. You can choose to deactivate the stick completely, activate the stick by pressing it, or keep it activated continually. For this book, we choose the latter option (ON) to ensure that the focus stick is always directly available.

■ Press the focus stick in shooting mode to access the focus frame and focus zone selection screen. Here, you can move the active focus frame or zone around with the focus stick and change its size by turning one of the command dials. In this selection screen, you can press the focus stick again to center the focus frame or zone.

■ In shooting mode, you can move the focus stick directly in eight directions to change the position of the active focus frame or zone. However, you can't change their size before pressing the focus stick.

■ In playback mode (while viewing an image), use the front command dial to browse through the images that are on file.

■ During playback, you can turn the rear command dial to zoom in and out of an image. By pressing the DISP/BACK button, you can always directly return to the standard-size view. Press the rear command dial to zoom into a 100% view of a shot. When you are zoomed-in, pressing the dial again returns the camera to its regular view, displaying the full image.

■ While displaying a RAW image in playback mode, you can press the Q button to directly access the built-in RAW converter. This function allows you to create new JPEG versions of your image with different settings.

■ In playback mode, press the upper selector button to view the first of two information pages that show additional shooting parameters and the position of the focus point. This function is not available in the FAVORITES display mode.

- In playback mode, you can use the focus stick as an alternative to the selector buttons and the MENU/OK button.

- Press and hold the playback button in playback mode to directly switch between the two memory card slots (while using two cards at the same time).

- For direct access to the format menu, press and hold the DELETE ("trash") button for about three seconds. Keep the DELETE button depressed and press the rear command dial.

TIP 28	Suggested Fn button assignment

Smart assignment of your X-T2's Fn buttons will save you many cumbersome trips to the camera menu. To display and change the assignment of all available Fn buttons in one convenient menu, press and hold the DISP/BACK button in shooting mode until the configuration page called Fn/AE-L/AF-L BUTTON SETTING appears.

Here are my suggested Fn button assignments:

- **Fn1: PERFORMANCE.** The Fn1 key is my "wild card", meaning I tend to put a frequently used function on it that helps me with the task at hand. Usually, this would be the PERFORMANCE function to quickly toggle the camera between Normal and Boost mode. In concert with the Vertical Power Booster Grip (which has its own dedicated Normal/Boost switch), Fn1 is free for other tasks, for example WHITE BALANCE or quick access the new FLASH FUNCTION SETTING page. I will also configure it as a TTL-LOCK button in concert with TTL flash photography.

- **Fn2: AF MODE.** Besides the switch at the front of the camera that allows you to choose between AF-S(ingle) and AF-C(ontinuous), there are three additional AF modes that can be combined with either AF-S or AF-C: SINGLE

POINT, ZONE, and WIDE/TRACKING. In order to quickly switch between these modes, it's useful to assign their selection to one of the Fn buttons. Personally, I prefer Fn2 (at the front of the camera) for this job.

- **Fn3: AF-C CUSTOM SETTINGS.** AF-C Custom Settings allow fine-tuning the X-T2 for action photography and everything that involves moving subjects. In situations like this, time is of the essence, which is why I want quick, direct access to this menu.

- **Fn4: Auto-ISO.** Since Auto-ISO is a very important and frequently used setting, it should be accessible via one of the Fn buttons. After all, there are three different Auto-ISO configurations to choose from.

- **Fn5: DYNAMIC RANGE.** Fujifilm cameras offer a very powerful and high-quality DR function to extend the highlight dynamic range of an image, so it's a good idea to keep this function right at your fingertips.

- **Fn6: FACE DETECTION.** Face Detection is another function that should be at your fingertips when it's required, so putting it on Fn6 makes perfect sense.

- **AF-L and AE-L:** In the X-T2, the AF-L and AE-L buttons also serve as Fn keys, so you can repurpose them if needed. That said, I don't tend to change their assignment, because I regard both AE-L and AF-L as useful functions. However, if you come from a DSLR and are used to its AF-ON (a.k.a. "back-button focusing") function, you might want to reassign the AF-L button to the X-T2's new AF-ON function.

Always shoot **FINE+RAW!**	TIP 29

The age-old question of whether to shoot RAW or JPEG [23] gives users of X-series cameras like the X-T2 a limited choice. The best option is using both formats by setting IMAGE QUALITY SETTING > IMAGE QUALITY > FINE+RAW. It doesn't matter if you consider yourself a diehard RAW shooter or a JPEG shooter.

This is how **diehard RAW shooters** benefit from shooting FINE+RAW:

- During external RAW processing, the camera-made JPEG can be used as a (sometimes hard-to-beat) reference image. Sometimes, users struggle to get better results with post-processing programs than they can get with the camera's default instant JPEG.

- Checking critical focus is only possible at 100% magnification, which only a high-resolution JPEG can provide. The JPEG that's embedded in the RAW file for preview purposes is too small. Make sure you select one of the three available L (Large) options under IMAGE QUALITY SETTING > IMAGE SIZE.

- The IMAGE SIZE menu isn't available in RAW-only mode. Different image formats, such as 1:1 or 16:9, are only available in JPEG-only mode or FINE+RAW mode. Autofocus and exposure metering adapt to the currently selected format (aspect ratio) and deliver more accurate readings when you are shooting with odd formats like 1:1. No worries, though: the RAW is always recorded in the sensor's native 3:2 format, so you don't lose any image information. Using the built-in RAW converter to generate a JPEG from a RAW file will always result in full-size 3:2 format JPEGs with maximum resolution.

This is how **diehard JPEG shooters** benefit from shooting FINE+RAW:

- Nobody is capable of always setting the *perfect* shooting parameters (exposure, white balance, dynamic range, as well as JPEG parameters such as film simulation, color, sharpness, noise reduction, shadow and highlight contrast, grain effect, etc.) in advance. FINE+RAW solves this problem by allowing you to change and adjust those settings after the fact, either with the built-in RAW converter or an external RAW converter. This means you can worry about those JPEG settings later and concentrate on more important factors of your shot, such as focus, framing, and timing.

■ Even if you chose the perfect settings in advance, it's possible that you'd like to have more than one version of a shot, such as a color version and a black-and-white version, or versions with different color film simulations. Again, FINE+RAW does the trick because you can use the built-in RAW converter to create (and compare) different JPEG versions of a shot.

■ There's always progress in the digital domain. Things that appear impossible today may be a reality in just a few years. It's perfectly feasible that the RAW converters of the future will be able to extract much better image quality from your RAW files than today's cameras and RAW processors. It pays to be prepared by archiving the digital negatives (aka RAW files) of your valuable shots. Storage space is cheap; some of your images may be priceless.

■ Your skills may improve as well! Several months or a few years from now, you may be much more comfortable using post-processing software than you are today. Wouldn't it be sad if you couldn't revisit great shots of the past and process them in a better way? Don't forget: only RAW files contain the complete information of an image. JPEGs are just a processed and compressed subset with limited latitude for post-processing. RAW files feature much better tonality and dynamic range. By the way, using the built-in RAW converter of the X-T2 isn't more complex or complicated than using the camera's JPEG settings in the IMAGE QUALITY SETTING menu (which should be familiar to you as a JPEG shooter).

As you can see, RAW+FINE is always the best and most flexible choice. However, the one detrimental aspect of using RAW+FINE is that it results in large amounts of data being recorded. This doesn't matter much in practical terms because the X-T2 features a fast processor that can quickly transfer large amounts of data to a memory card. Just make sure to use a fast card!

Let me use this opportunity to address a widespread misconception: RAW files aren't images that you can directly look at. RAWs contain image *data* that still has to be *translated* or *processed* into an actual image—either in-camera or with external software. Every actual digital image (including the live view on the monitor, JPEGs from the camera, or TIFF files from Adobe Lightroom) is the result of such a translation.

A diehard JPEG shooter who doesn't keep RAW files has to settle for only one of the many possible translations of RAW data into an image, and it's highly unlikely that this single JPEG from the camera is the best of all possible versions of the image. Basically, discarding the RAW file turns the X-T2 into an instant camera: you only get one (most likely not the best) image per shot.

TIP 30	Compressed or uncompressed RAW files?

The X-T2 offers you a choice of uncompressed and compressed RAW files (IMAGE QUALITY SETTING > RAW RECORDING). Compression cuts the size of RAW files roughly in half, so you can store more of them on a memory card or your computer. The compression also helps speed up camera processes: it takes longer to fill the fast camera buffer, and since the files are smaller, they take less time to transfer to the memory card.

It's important to note that Fujifilm's RAW compression is lossless, so there's no difference in image quality between uncompressed and compressed RAWs. However, not all external RAW converters may be able to process compressed RAWs, because the compression format is proprietary. RAW converter manufacturers can obtain a free SDK from Fujifilm in order to support the compressed RAW file format.

Pick a suitable **image format**!	TIP 31

The full resolution of the X-T2 (about 24 megapixels) is only available in its native image format (3:2). However, using a different image format (such as 1:1 or 16:9) can still be reasonable. For example, some people prefer to view their images on a 16:9 HD television, while others are fans of the classic (square) medium format look.

No matter what format (aspect ratio) and resolution you choose in IMAGE QUALITY SETTING > IMAGE SIZE, it will only affect the JPEGs coming from your camera. RAW files are always recorded in full resolution in the native 3:2 sensor format. This means that as long as you kept your RAW files, you can generate new full-size 3:2-format JPEGs with the built-in RAW converter or an external RAW processor.

If you want to compose shots in the 1:1 or 16:9 formats, you should select the desired format in the shooting menu. Here's why:

- The live view in the viewfinder or on the LCD will automatically adjust to the new format, making it easier to compose an image.

- The camera's autofocus frames will adapt to the selected image format.

- The camera's exposure metering and live histogram are based on what's displayed in the live view. Changing the live view to 16:9 or 1:1 will enhance metering accuracy for the respective format.

TIP 32 | The magical half-press

A basic rule for successfully using mirrorless cameras like the X-T2 is minimizing the delay between pressing the shutter button and the camera actually taking the image. It's all about not missing the decisive moment due to shutter lag.

It's up to you to anticipate these decisive moments. You should have the shutter button already half-pressed so you're ready to fully depress it to actually take the shot. By half-pressing the shutter button, you are preparing the camera: exposure and autofocus (unless you are using AF-C) will be set and locked, and the lens aperture will move to its working position. The camera is now ready to record an image with minimal shutter lag—all that's left to do is to fully depress the already half-pressed shutter button at the right instant.

Don't forget that priming the camera by half-pressing the shutter only works if SHUTTER AE and SHUTTER AF are both set to ON in the SET UP > BUTTON DIAL SETTING menu.

2.2 MONITOR AND VIEWFINDER

The X-T2 features a large, high-resolution electronic viewfinder (EVF) along with an LCD monitor. Both can be used for image composition and playback.

TIP 33 | Make use of the **eye sensor!**

Use the VIEW MODE button to activate the built-in eye sensor. The camera will now automatically switch to whichever view (viewfinder or rear LCD screen) is in use when you are taking or reviewing images (or making changes to the camera menu).

When you are working with a tripod or holding the LCD display close to your body, the eye sensor can get confused. In such cases, use the VIEW MODE button to set the camera to LCD ONLY.

Instant review	TIP 34

To instantly review an image right after you have taken it, you can select SET UP > SCREEN SET-UP > IMAGE DISP. and then set a display period of 0.5 SEC, 1.5 SEC, or CONTINUOUS. The image will always be displayed in the currently active view (LCD or viewfinder).

You can immediately cancel an image review to continue shooting by half-pressing the shutter button. With the CONTINUOUS option, you can also zoom into the image: pressing the rear command dial will directly zoom to the highest available magnification.

In situations that require you to take a series of shots in quick succession, it may be advisable to switch image review off. To do so, select SET UP > SCREEN SET-UP > IMAGE DISP. > OFF. With image review off, you can still check your latest shot by pressing the playback button.

Please don't forget that the maximum magnification (to check critical focus) is only available when the camera is set to record RAW *and* JPEG files in size L.

The **DISP/BACK button** can be tricky!	TIP 35

The DISP/BACK button serves two different purposes:

■ As a BACK button, it returns the camera to a higher menu or selection level without saving any changes you may have made in the menu sub-level.

■ As a DISPLAY button, it changes the display mode of the currently active view (LCD monitor or viewfinder).

It's important to remember that changing the display mode only affects the currently active view. For example, in order to change the display mode of the EVF, the EVF must be in use when you press the DISP/BACK button. This means that when you are using the eye sensor, you must actually look through the EVF while you are pressing the DISP/BACK button. If you don't, you will only change the display mode of the LCD monitor.

When the camera is in shooting mode, the viewfinder and the LCD monitor can each use different display modes at the same time.

In playback mode, the EVF and LCD are synched to the same display mode. In this case it doesn't matter which view (EVF or LCD) is active when you change the display mode with the DISP/BACK button.

If you select a display with information overlays in shooting mode, you can choose which elements will appear in the viewfinder or on the LCD monitor. Select SET UP > SCREEN SET-UP > DISP. CUSTOM SETTING, and then check the items that you want displayed in the EVF and on the LCD. I recommend you check all items on the list.

| TIP 36 | WYSIWYG—What You See Is What You Get! |

The EVF and LCD monitor of the X-T2 operate in WYSIWYG mode [24]: What You See Is What You Get. This means that the viewfinder and monitor are always trying to display a live view [25] image that closely resembles how the resulting JPEG will look. The live view simulates exposure, colors, contrast, and white balance. Plus, when you half-press the shutter, the camera will set the selected working aperture, so the live view will also display a preview of the depth of field.

The live view's exposure simulation is quite helpful because it allows you to recognize exposure errors before you take the picture. Please note that the live histogram is always based on the current live view image.

The live view's WYSIWYG simulation is available in all four of the camera's exposure modes: program AE **P**, aperture priority **A**, shutter priority **S**, and manual exposure mode **M**.

In manual mode **M**, you can switch the exposure simulation off by selecting SET UP > SCREEN SET-UP > PREVIEW EXP./WB IN MANUAL MODE > OFF. That way, the X-T2 will always display a bright live view image in manual mode, regardless of the chosen exposure parameters (shutter speed, aperture, and ISO). This can be useful in a studio setting with flash photography. For example, you may want to eliminate the surrounding light component by stopping down the aperture and fully illuminating your subject with flashguns.

Please note that both the live view and the live histogram aren't representing the actual exposure in this mode, so don't forget to switch the exposure simulation back on with SET UP > SCREEN SET-UP > PREVIEW EXP./WB IN MANUAL MODE > PREVIEW EXP./WB if you want to work with a proper exposure simulation and live histogram in manual mode **M**.

The live view's exposure simulation is limited in situations with very low light and slow shutter speeds of several seconds. In these cases, the live view and the live histogram may appear darker than the actual result. In such scenarios, you should first take a test shot and review it in playback mode. The information display (which you can select with the DISP/BACK button) will show you a playback histogram of the recorded JPEG image. This includes a preview with "blinkies," which indicate blown (overexposed) highlights. Sadly, the playback histogram only shows the picture's luminance (overall brightness distribution), not its three distinct RGB color channels.

| TIP 37 | Using the **Natural Live View** |

The so-called Natural Live View is a display mode that disables the WYSIWYG simulation of JPEG settings such as Film Simulation, Highlight Tone, Shadow Tone, or Color. Instead, it will display a live view image with increased dynamic range in the highlights and shadows, and with natural colors that are supposed to resemble what our eyes would see through an optical viewfinder. It will also set the live view to Auto white balance, so there will be no simulation of any white balance settings or presets in the live view. However, all current JPEG and white balance settings will still be applied to the *actual image* that's recorded.

To set the camera to Natural Live View mode, select SET UP > SCREEN SET-UP > PREVIEW PIC. EFFECT > OFF. This setting enables generic-looking previews for color, black-and-white, and sepia shots that do *not* reflect the look of the actual JPEG results. This makes Natural Live View particularly useful: you can see what's going on in the dark parts of a high-contrast scene while composing the shot.

Important: The Natural Live View of the X-T2 extends highlight dynamic range by two stops, rendering the live histogram inaccurate when shooting with DR100%, DR200%, or DR-Auto dynamic range settings.

2.3 EXPOSING RIGHT

It's not the job of the camera to find and set the right exposure; it's the job of the photographer. That said, the X-T2 features the usual set of AE (auto exposure) modes: aperture priority **A**, shutter priority **S**, and program AE **P**.

- **Aperture priority** `A` will automatically set a suitable shutter speed to match a preset aperture based on your exposure.

- **Shutter priority** `S` will automatically set a suitable aperture to match a preset shutter speed based on your exposure.

- **Program AE** `P` will automatically set a suitable aperture and shutter speed combination based on your exposure.

- **Auto-ISO** can contribute a suitable ISO setting (within predefined limits). In digital cameras, ISO is the level of signal amplification applied to an image that has been recorded by the camera's sensor. ISO impacts the brightness of the final image.

It is important to understand that these auto exposure (AE) modes (including Auto-ISO) are not responsible for correctly exposing images; exposure is always the responsibility of the photographer. AE modes automatically fill variables (such as the shutter speed in aperture priority `A`) in a way that matches the exposure you've set manually. Auto exposure will only deliver good results if the photographer is exposing correctly.

Exposing correctly—how does this work?

Don't panic! Unlike conventional DSLR cameras, the mirrorless X-T2 makes things easy. Four different metering modes (multi, spot, center-weighted, and average), the WYSIWYG live view, and the live histogram help you find the correct exposure for any given scene. The most important tool is the exposure compensation dial, which allows you to correct the metered exposure up to ±3 EV in convenient steps of 1/3 EV. EV means Exposure Value, and 1 EV is equivalent to one full aperture stop. The correct exposure isn't what the camera is metering; it's what *you* make of the metering by adjusting the exposure compensation dial.

| TIP 38 | Choosing the right **metering method** |

There are four different metering methods available to measure the amount of light that goes through the lens and hits the image sensor.

- **Average** metering calculates an unweighted average of the total light that hits the entire sensor area.

- **Spot** metering only considers two percent of the sensor area. The metering area covers a medium-sized autofocus frame in the center of the image. Alternatively, you can link spot metering to the size and position of the active autofocus frame (in SINGLE POINT AF and MF mode).

- **Center-weighted** metering is a crossbreed between average and spot metering. While it encompasses the entire image area, it puts special emphasis on the image center.

- **Multi** or **matrix** metering calculates a weighted average of the total light that hits the sensor. The weight is a result of 256 metering areas (the matrix) that the camera evaluates and compares to typical scenarios, which is why multi metering is considered "smarter" than the other methods. For example, multi metering is designed to recognize when you are shooting against the sun.

Average, spot and center-weighted metering return exposure recommendations based on middle gray. In other words, when you take a picture of a black wall and then a picture of a white wall, the results will both look middle gray. This means:

- If you want the black wall to actually look black in the resulting image, you have to manually adjust the exposure downward.

- If you want the white wall to actually look bright white in the resulting image, you have to manually adjust the exposure upward.

Fig. 21: This illustration shows a black sheet of paper and a white sheet of paper. Both were photographed with the camera's spot metering without any exposure correction. As you can see, the camera delivered a **middle-gray exposure** in both cases. In order to get an image that reflects the actual brightness of the subject, the metered exposure has to be adjusted.

Fujifilm recommends a correction of +1 EV when you are shooting in snowfields, or −2/3 EV when you are shooting subjects in spotlight. Instead of these rules, I recommend a more precise and methodical course of action using the live view and the live histogram. To minimize corrective adjustments, it's best to select a metering method that fits the subject or the job at hand:

- **Multi** metering is a general-purpose method. Since it is supposed to be "smarter" than the other methods, there's a good chance that you won't have to apply any corrective adjustments to the proposed exposure.

- **Average** and, to a lesser degree, **center-weighted** metering are rather neutral metering methods that will likely stay more consistent despite small changes in composition (or framing) than multi metering and spot metering. I recommend average metering if you want to take a series of shots of the same subjects under similar conditions. In such cases, average metering will help you keep the exposure consistent.

- **Spot** metering bases its measurements on one particular spot of the overall image. This means you have to work very precisely to make sure you are metering the appropriate part (spot) of the scene. The resulting exposure recommendation will expose this spot with middle-gray brightness. For example, if you spot meter a backlit face against the sun, the metered exposure will display the face with middle-gray brightness (or zone 5 in the famous Ansel Adams zone system [26]). If that's too dark for your taste, you can use the exposure compensation dial to lift the exposure by +1/3 EV or +2/3 EV. On the other hand, if the person has dark skin, you may want to reduce the exposure with a correction in the opposite direction. It's up to you to choose the zone (brightness) of the spot-metered part of the image.

Spot metering is the most powerful and challenging metering method. It's useful when the light is very difficult—too difficult for multi and average metering. Typical examples are isolated bright objects in front of a dark background (and vice versa), such as a musician or an actor on a stage, or strongly backlit subjects. Whenever your exposure has to be spot on, spot metering is your friend.

With that said, it's pretty obvious that spot metering requires you to meter very precisely. Even small changes in the cameras direction can lead to dramatic changes in the metered result. This is why it can be useful to combine spot metering with the camera's AE-L button. AE-L will lock your exposure to prevent it from changing as soon as you alter your composition or your subject starts to move away from your metering spot.

Alternatively, you can use spot metering in manual mode **M**. In this mode, metering doesn't affect the exposure because you are setting all the exposure parameters (shutter speed, aperture, and ISO) manually. Spot metering in manual mode helps you determine the brightness level (zone) of any part of your image for any given exposure. The exposure scale in the viewfinder or LCD tells you exactly how much brighter or darker than middle gray (zone 5) the spot metered object would appear in your shot (±3 EV).

Don't forget to *disable* Auto-ISO in manual mode **M**. If you don't, the camera will still operate in some kind of AE mode (I call it "misomatic"); in this mode, the ISO setting will be the exposure variable that's automatically adjusted.

Linking spot metering to AF frames	TIP 39

Traditionally, spot metering covers the center of the frame with an area that's about as large as a medium-sized (standard) focus frame. However, by selecting AF/MF SET-TING > INTERLOCK SPOT AE & FOCUS AREA > ON, you can link the spot metering area to the position and size(!) of the active autofocus frame in Single Point AF.

This is a very useful feature if you are using one of the camera's other AF frames that *aren't* in the center, since it's likely that your focus area covers the same part of your subject that is also relevant for exposure metering (such as the brightly lit face of a stage actor who is standing in front of a dark background).

If you want to decouple spot metering from the AF area and limit it to the very center of the frame, make sure to select AF/MF SETTING > INTERLOCK SPOT AE & FOCUS AREA > OFF.

Please note that the camera will not interlock spot metering with the focus area if you set the camera to either Zone AF or Wide/Tracking AF. Interlocking only works in concert with Single Point AF or manual focus (MF) mode.

Using the **live view and live histogram**	TIP 40

Unlike optical viewfinders in DSLRs, the electronic live view of the X-T2 provides a pretty good simulation of the resulting image. The live preview encompasses colors, contrast, and exposure.

In standard display mode, this WYSIWYG preview is complemented by a live histogram. I strongly recommend using the live histogram because it provides a useful overview of the brightness distribution in your scene. It also helps you identify areas of over- and underexposure in advance, so you can take corrective measures:

- If bars are piling up like a bell curve at the right end of the histogram, but cut off mid-peak, parts of your shot will be overexposed with blown highlights. If this affects important parts of your image, you should correct the exposure downward. Alternately, you can expand the camera's dynamic range by selecting DR200% or DR400% in the respective menu.

- If the histogram leans to the left, leaving plenty of space on the right, the shot might end up underexposed. In this case, you can adjust the exposure upward.

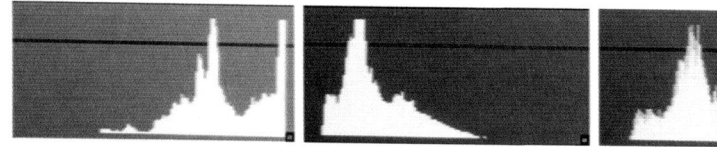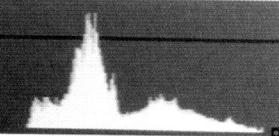

Fig. 22: Different **live histograms** showing a tendency for over-exposure, underexposure, and a balanced exposure of the same scene.

The histogram provides a technical representation of the live view simulation. As long as the Natural Live View is turned off, both the live view and the live histogram will reflect the current JPEG settings of the camera (white balance, film simulation, color, and highlight and shadow contrast). For example, the VELVIA film simulation will deliver more contrast than PROVIA, and this will be reflected in the live view and the live histogram.

It's important to note that the live view and live histogram now also represent manual DR200% or DR400% settings. However, if you set the camera to DR-Auto, the live view and live histogram will always show a DR100% preview.

When you half-press the shutter, the camera's live view will always try to give you an accurate representation of the resulting image's dynamic range. That said, there is no live histogram when you half-press the shutter, so you'll have to fully rely on the visual impression provided by the live view image.

Auto exposure (AE) with modes **P**, **A**, and **S**	**TIP 41**

P (program AE), **A** (aperture priority), and **S** (shutter priority) are the three auto exposure modes of your X-T2.

A brief reminder:

- **Program AE P** will automatically set a suitable aperture and shutter-speed combination.

- **Aperture priority A** will automatically set a suitable shutter speed to match a preset aperture.

- **Shutter priority S** will automatically set a suitable aperture to match a preset shutter speed.

To take a picture in one of these modes, you can follow these steps:

- Meter the exposure with one of the metering modes: multi, center-weighted, average, or spot.

- After metering, adjust the exposure to taste using the exposure compensation dial. Use the live view and the histogram to determine the best corrections. Remember: it's not the camera that's setting the exposure; it's you. Don't blindly follow what the camera is proposing. Instead, always keep an eye on the live view and the live histogram.

- When you half-press the shutter button, your exposure will be locked as long as you keep the button half-depressed. This means that as long as the shutter button

is half-pressed, you can adjust the framing or composition of your shot without changing the exposure.

■ Instead of half-pressing the shutter button, you can
also use the AE-L button to meter a scene and lock the
exposure. You can configure the AE-L button to either
lock the exposure as long as you press the AF-L button
(SET UP > BUTTON/DIAL SETTING > AE/AF LOCK MODE >
AE&AF ON WHEN PRESSING), or use the button as a toggle to lock and unlock the exposure (SET UP > BUTTON/
DIAL SETTING > AE/AF LOCK MODE > AE&AF ON/OFF
SWITCH). When the exposure is locked with AE-L, you
can still correct it with the exposure compensation dial.

■ To take the shot, fully depress the shutter button.

Metering and exposure are two different things. After metering a scene, the photographer sets the actual exposure
with the exposure compensation dial:

■ **Metering** is performed using either multi, center-
weighted, average, or spot metering.

■ Use the **exposure compensation dial** to adjust the metering result. Use the information from the live view and
live histogram to adjust your settings. Of course, there
are many instances where the initial metering is already
spot-on, so you won't have to apply any further correction.

■ **Expose** the image using one of three AE modes: aperture
priority, shutter priority, or program AE.

TIP 42	Using manual exposure **M**

In manual mode, you manually specify all three exposure
parameters: aperture, shutter speed, and ISO amplification.
In order for this to work, Auto-ISO has to be turned off. Otherwise, ISO would become an exposure variable that the
camera would automatically fill.

For the live view and live histogram to correctly display the set exposure in manual mode, make sure that SET UP > SCREEN SET-UP > PREVIEW EXP./WB IN MANUAL MODE > PREVIEW EXP./WB is set. I recommend setting the metering to spot metering.

Here's how you can expose in manual mode:

■ Select and set an aperture and shutter speed that suits your subject and image idea. Aperture controls the depth of field [27]; shutter speed controls the amount of motion blur [11] in your exposure.

■ Next, select an ISO value that will yield the desired brightness in your shot. You can (and should) use the live view and live histogram to find a suitable setting. As usual, try not to blow out important highlights. The live histogram is your friend.

■ You can check specific parts of your scene by spot metering them. The exposure scale in the live view screen tells you how much above or below middle gray (zone 5) the spot metered selection will be exposed. This tool helps you ensure that important parts of your image (such as skin tones) will be exposed exactly like you want them to be.

■ Finally, you may want to readjust or fine-tune aperture, shutter speed, and ISO according to your metering. Once everything is set, you can take the shot(s).

Using **aperture priority** A	**TIP 43**

In aperture priority AE [28], you manually set the aperture [29], and the camera automatically selects a suitable shutter speed based on your chosen exposure (as set with the exposure compensation dial). Which aperture should you select? Let's look at some basics:

- As the aperture gets smaller (the aperture number gets higher), your depth of field [27] (DOF) increases. DOF is the zone in front of and behind the focus plane that appears in perfect focus in your resulting image. In standard display mode, the viewfinder and LCD offer a focus and DOF bar that displays the focus distance and the calculated depth-of-field zone that surrounds it.

- Fast lenses like the XF56mmF1.2 or the XF35mmF1.4 often exhibit a tight DOF of less than an inch when used wide open, so it's possible, for instance, in a portrait shot, for only one of the subject's eyes to be perfectly in focus. If that's the case, you can stop down the lens or change the position of your subject so that both eyes are exactly the same distance from the camera.

- Stopping down a lens beyond f/10 leads to increased diffraction blur [14] across the image area. While the larger depth of field increases the in-focus zone, maximum detail is reduced. In other words, when you shoot with f/22 using a wide-angle lens, there's a good chance that your scene will be in focus from front to back. However, its overall crispness will be lower than it would be at f/8. The Lens Modulation Optimizer (LMO) in your X-T2 can compensate for diffraction blur to a degree, but its effect only extends to JPEGs from the camera, including those created by the built-in RAW converter. External RAW converters don't support the LMO.

- When you shoot wide open or with a high ISO setting, it's possible that the suitable shutter speed is faster than the camera's maximum speed of 1/8000s. If that's the case, the shutter speed will be displayed in red (overexposure warning). You can use shutter speeds beyond 1/8000s by engaging the camera's electronic shutter.

Using **shutter priority** S

Shutter priority [30] AE works like aperture priority, ex-cept you are manually setting a shutter speed [31], and the camera automatically selects a fitting aperture value based on your exposure. Shutter priority is only available when you're using native X-mount lenses with electronic contacts. Adapted lenses can only be used with aperture priority or in manual mode.

Setting the right shutter speed is dependent on two factors:

- Motion blur [11]: The faster your subject is moving, the faster your shutter speed has to be in order to avoid shots with motion blur. This doesn't mean that motion blur is always bad; it can be used as a conscious choice to add dynamic punch to your image. For instance, panning [12] the camera blurs the background behind a sharp main subject. Motion blur can be a benefit of long exposures [32]—exposure times of several seconds or minutes can smoothen water surfaces, blur cloudy skies, or add star trails.

- Blur due to camera shake [33]: if you don't hold the cam-era steady when you take a shot, the resulting image can be blurred. The optical image stabilizer [10] (OIS) of the XC and XF zoom lenses can help, or you can put the camera on a tripod or a solid surface and use the self-timer or a remote shutter release to take the shot. A rule of thumb suggests using at least the reciprocal of the (35mm equiv-alent) focal length as your shutter speed. For example, if you are using a 200mm lens on your X-T2 (and the OIS has been switched off), your minimum shutter speed should be 1/300s, since you have to multiply the focal length with the APS-C crop factor [09] of 1.5. Of course, rules of thumb don't apply to every situation. It really depends on your technique and whether or not you're blessed with steady hands.

If you set a very slow shutter speed or choose a high ISO setting, it's possible that even the smallest aperture opening of your lens will still be too large to avoid overexposure. In this case, the aperture value will be displayed in red.

You can quickly change the shutter speed in full-stop increments using the shutter speed dial. You can also use the command dial to fine-tune your selection in 1/3 EV intermediate steps.

*Hint: Setting the shutter dial to **T** (Time) allows you to select the **full** range of available shutter speeds (in 1/3 EV steps) by turning the front command dial. (Make sure that SET UP > BUTTON/DIAL SETTING > COMMAND DIAL SETTING > S.S. F is selected.)*

TIP 45	Using **program AE** **P** **and program shift**

In program AE, the camera will automatically pick a combination of aperture *and* shutter speed settings that correspond to your chosen exposure. This mode can be useful for inexperienced photographers or in situations when you don't have the time to manually adjust the aperture or shutter speed.

In program AE, the slowest possible shutter speed is 4 seconds. When this is not sufficiently slow for the shot you are attempting (in concert with a wide-open aperture), the camera will display a red underexposure warning.

Even in program AE, you can influence shutter speed and aperture to a degree by using program shift [34]. Program shift allows you to select a better combination of aperture and shutter speed than the one originally proposed by the camera's program AE. You can cycle through different combinations of apertures and shutter speeds that all result in the same exposure. Use program shift by turning the front command dial.

Important: *Program shift is only available when certain conditions are met: it's not available if Dynamic Range is set to AUTO or if a TTL flash unit is in use.*

Playing it safe with **auto exposure bracketing**	TIP 46

As you know by now, the automatic exposure (AE) modes **P**, **A**, and **S** are merely responsible for selecting the correct exposure parameters. The exposure itself is the responsibility of the photographer. You can use metering (multi, center-weighted, average, or spot), the live view, and the live histogram to determine the right exposure.

Nobody is perfect! If you want to play it safe, auto exposure bracketing [35] can be a helpful feature. In this mode (set the DRIVE dial to BKT and select SHOOTING SETTING > DRIVE SETTING > BKT SETTING > BKT SELECT > AE BKT), the camera takes a series of three shots in quick succession, each with a different exposure: one shot with normal exposure, one underexposed shot, and one overexposed shot. You can set a bracketing spread of up to ±2 EV in the BKT SETTING menu.

Exposure bracketing is especially useful with subjects that don't move. After you've taken the shot, you can decide which of the three differently exposed versions you want to keep.

Long exposures	TIP 47

Long exposures can lead to impressive results. Fireworks, night shots, interesting water surfaces, stars, or clouds: exposure times of several seconds or minutes capture the course of time in a single photograph. Of course, this only works if you put the camera on a tripod or a solid surface.

You have two basic options:

- Set the shutter-speed dial to **T** (Time) and then use the front command dial to set the shutter speed. In order to avoid camera shake, use a remote shutter release or the self-timer to take the shot.

- Set the shutter speed dial to **B** (Bulb), then press and hold the shutter for as long as you want the camera to expose. Obviously, it makes sense to use a remote shutter release that can be locked for the duration of the shot.

For good-quality results, make sure to set IMAGE QUALITY SETTING > LONG EXPOSURE NR > ON. By doing so, the camera will perform a dark-frame subtraction [22] depending on what ISO and exposure time you used. Dark-frame subtraction doubles the effective exposure duration, so be patient.

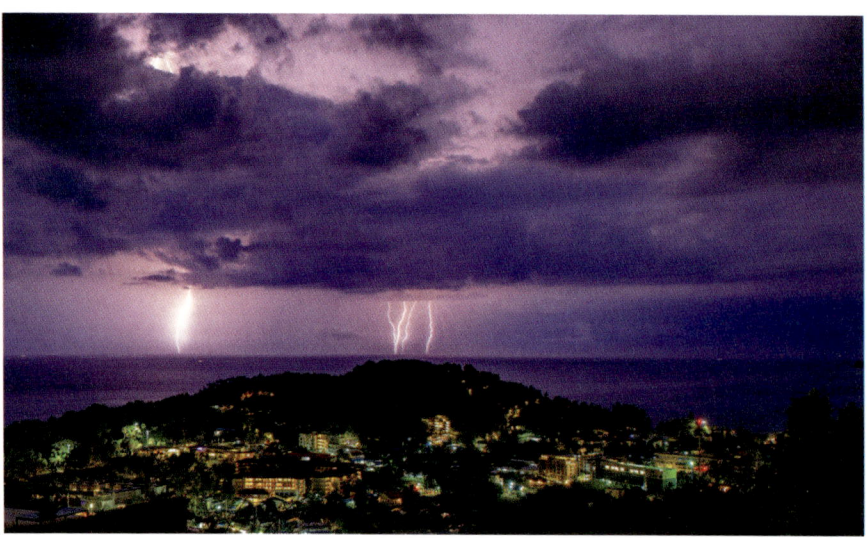

Fig. 23: A **long exposure** of 30 seconds taken in T mode. Make sure to use a tripod for these kinds of shots.

Long exposures in bright daylight	TIP 48

In order to achieve long exposure times under normal daylight conditions, you can't just stop down the lens—even at f/22, your shutter speed would still be too fast. Besides, diffraction blur is kicking it beyond f/10, so stopping down beyond this point is only recommended when it cannot be avoided.

To realize long shutter speeds in good light, it's best to use a so-called ND filter [36], or neutral density filter. This is a fancy name for a simple gray filter that you can put in front of the lens to block a portion of the light from reaching the sensor.

For example, a filter with an ND 3.0 specification will extend your exposure time by a factor of about 1000 (or 10 f-stops). This means that by using such a filter, a scene that would normally require a shutter speed of 1/50s at f/8 can be shot at the same aperture with an exposure time of 20 seconds.

However, there's a catch: since your X-T2 is equipped with a rather weak infrared cut filter in front of the sensor, long exposures (typically one minute or longer) in bright daylight should be performed with a regular neutral density (ND) filter and a dedicated IR cut filter in front of the lens. This will help you avoid false colors. A few ND filters already include an IR cut filter.

ISO settings—what's the deal?	TIP 49

The meaning of ISO in the digital realm is often misunderstood. Higher ISO settings *don't* increase the sensor's sensitivity. The sensor in your X-T2 is calibrated to its native ISO 200 (based on the popular SOS standard) [37], and this remains the same no matter what ISO you set in the camera.

To be clear, there's no difference between taking a shot with f/5.6 and 1/60s at either ISO 100 or at ISO 25600. In both cases the sensor is exposed to the exact same amount of light (or photons). The amount of light (the real exposure) is solely determined by aperture and shutter speed.

So what exactly is ISO doing? ISO determines the amount of *signal amplification* that's applied to the image. ISO 200, the sensor's native setting, is equivalent to the camera's basic calibration. At ISO 400, the signal (or sensor data) is amplified by one aperture stop to brighten the image and increase its exposure. At ISO 800, the amplification amounts to two stops, and so on. At ISO 25600, the additional amplification of the light recorded by the sensor amounts to seven stops. It's not surprising that image quality decreases when ISO amplification increases; noise and artifacts are amplified along with the actual image data.

The amplification we are talking about means brightening the image by increasing its exposure. If you are familiar with external RAW converters such as Lightroom, you know there's an exposure slider. Moving this slider to the left or right changes the exposure (and hence the ISO) of an image. So the concept of ISO amplification isn't limited to the camera itself—it's part of the entire workflow from exposure via RAW file (digital negative) to the final JPEG or TIFF file (digital print).

If you take a shot with an ISO 800 setting, you're telling the camera to expose the image two stops darker than it would at its base ISO of 200, then amplify (brighten) that image two stops to compensate for the underexposure.

Regarding image quality and ISO, there's a basic rule: lower ISO settings lead to higher-quality results—hence the general recommendation to keep the ISO settings as low as possible. However, we obviously can't shoot with ISO 200 all the time, especially in low-light situations.

There are two basic methods to amplify a digital image:

- **Analog/digital hybrid amplification** *prior* **to writing the RAW file:** This method applies a mix of analog and digital signal processing to amplify or push the image to the brightness level that corresponds to the ISO setting. The digitized result of this process is then saved as a RAW file.

- **Digital amplification (push)** *after* **writing the RAW file:** This method changes the brightness of an image during RAW processing, *after* the RAW file has been written. The metadata (aka instructions) in the RAW file will tell the RAW converter what to do. You can also use your X-T2's built-in RAW converter to adjust the brightness (and hence, ISO) of an image after it's been recorded, or by moving your external RAW converter's exposure slider.

Digital amplification during RAW processing is beneficial because it's reversible. If the amplification (exposure) is too strong, you can always adjust it. ISO (aka exposure amplification) is a volatile aspect of the photography process because it can be changed anytime: in-camera, prior to writing the RAW file, or later during RAW processing.

The sensor in your X-T2 is a so-called ISOless sensor. This means there's no relevant quality difference between conventional signal amplification prior to writing a RAW file and digital amplification later during RAW conversion. This is great, because it allows you to digitally increase the ISO (aka brightness/exposure) of your shots during RAW processing, either in-camera or with external software such as Lightroom. Pushing the exposure up later in Lightroom won't look any different than choosing a higher ISO setting when you take the shot.

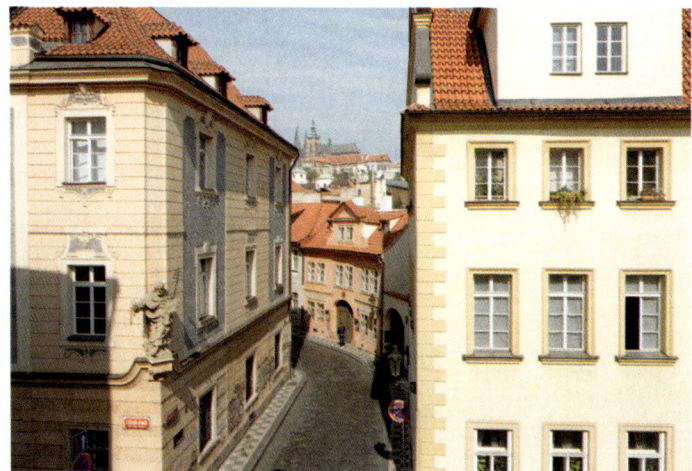

Fig. 24: **ISOless sensor (1):** This shot was taken at ISO 1600, with classic analog/digital in-camera amplification from base-ISO 200 to ISO 1600. The ISO 1600 result was then burned into the RAW file.

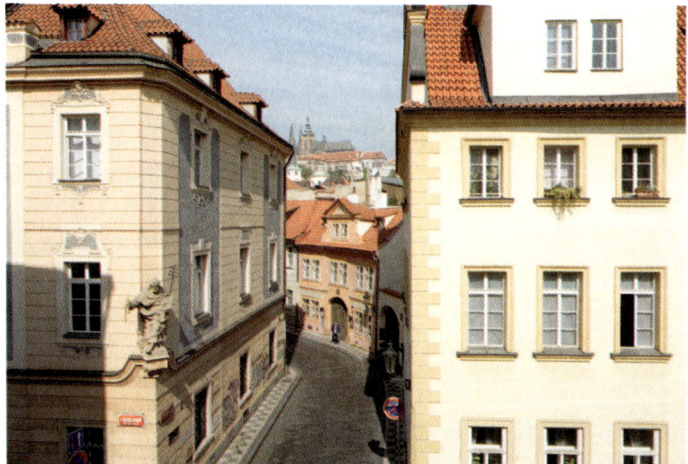

Fig. 25: **ISOless sensor (2):** This shot was also effectively taken at ISO 1600. However, the amplification from ISO 200 to ISO 1600 took place digitally during RAW conversion by moving the exposure slider three stops to the right. You won't be able to see any quality difference between the two shots in this book, so I invite you to take a look at full-size samples that are uploaded to Flickr. You can access the sample album here [38].

| What you should know about **extended** ISO | TIP 50 |

You will probably have noticed that in addition to the standard ISO settings (ISO 200 to ISO 12800), your X-T2 offers three additional settings: L (100), H (25600), and H (51200).

- **H means High:** In these modes, image data is further digitally amplified. In the case of ISO 51200, the last amplification stop is performed during RAW conversion. This enormous amplification leads to a visible decrease in quality. While ISO 25600 is still quite usable (especially for black and white JPEGs using the ACROS film simulation), ISO 51200 is only for emergencies.

- **L means LOW:** In this mode, an ISO 200 RAW that has been overexposed by one stop is pulled down one stop and saved, resulting in ISO 100 RAW and JPEG files. A digital pull is the direct opposite of a digital push operation: digital pull decreases the exposure of the resulting image. The ISO 100 RAW and JPEG files contain one stop *less* dynamic range than normal ISO 200 files. This means that bright areas like clouds in the sky can easily appear blown out. On the other hand, ISO 100 can add contrast and punch to scenes with dull lighting and little contrast.

| **Auto-ISO** and minimum shutter speed | TIP 51 |

You can automate the task of selecting the best (or lowest) ISO setting possible for any given shooting situation. Auto-ISO is an option with three configurable presets (AUTO1, AUTO2, and AUTO3) in the corresponding menu (SHOOTING SETTING > ISO AUTO SETTING):

- DEFAULT SENSITIVITY: This is the lower ISO limit. The camera will always try to use this ISO setting as long as the other parameters allow it.

■ MAX. SENSITIVITY: This is the upper ISO limit. The camera's Auto-ISO will never go beyond this point.

■ MIN. SHUTTER SPEED: Auto-ISO will automatically increase the ISO setting (up to the MAX. SENSITIVITY threshold) when the minimum shutter speed cannot be realized.

Obviously, MIN. SHUTTER SPEED is only relevant in auto exposure (AE) modes **A** and **P**, because the shutter speed is set manually in modes **M** and **S**. Auto-ISO makes sure that within the lower and upper ISO limits, the camera will always use a shutter speed that is at least as fast as the set minimal shutter speed.

Here's an example: let's say you are shooting in mode **A** (aperture priority) in bright light conditions using f/5.6. Auto-ISO is set to ISO 200 as the lower limit and ISO 12800 as the upper limit. You have set 1/125s as your minimum shutter speed, because you want to avoid motion blur while taking pictures of people walking in the street.

As long as the scene is brightly lit, there is no problem. The camera will use ISO 200 with shutter speeds at least as fast as 1/125s. However, as the sun sets and it becomes impossible to successfully use 1/125s at f/5.6 and ISO 200, Auto-ISO will increase the ISO to ensure that the shutter speed doesn't drop below 1/125s. This continues as the light conditions deteriorate until Auto-ISO reaches the upper ISO limit (in our case, ISO 12800). What now? Since the camera can't increase the ISO any further, it will start to reduce the shutter speed to values slower than 1/125s in order to still ensure a correct exposure.

In mode **S** (shutter priority), the photographer sets the shutter speed. In this mode, Auto-ISO will increase the ISO setting only when the aperture is already wide open. This can be a problem with fast lenses like the XF56mmF1.2, XF35mmF1.4, or XF23mmF1.4. When shot wide open, the depth of field of these lenses is quite limited (to say the least). That's why Auto-ISO is better used in modes **P** or **A**, at least in concert with fast lenses.

You can read more about Auto-ISO in my X-Pert Corner column here [39].

Auto-ISO in manual mode **M**: the "misomatic"	TIP 52

Manual mode in concert with Auto-**ISO** turns into another auto**MATIC** exposure mode: the so-called "**misomatic.**" In this mode, you preselect the aperture and shutter speed, and the camera automatically selects a suitable ISO setting that matches the exposure that has been determined by the currently active metering mode (multi, average, center-weighted, or spot).

To be useful in a misomatic application, Auto-ISO should be able to use the full ISO bandwidth, so you should config-ure it with a lower limit of ISO 200 and an upper limit of ISO 12800.

You have full manual control over aperture (depth of field) and shutter speed (motion blur and camera shake). You can tailor shutter speed and aperture to the requirements of the task at hand; there will be no surprises. At the same time, you still enjoy the comfort of automatic exposure (AE).

Misomatic also allows you to adjust the camera-metered exposure with the exposure compensation dial. For this to be effective, it's even more important to set the Auto-ISO DEFAULT SENSITIVITY to 200 and MAX. SENSITIVITY to 12800.

If you don't want to spend time with exposure compen-sation while you are in misomatic mode, you can use Fuji's DR function as a workaround by selecting DR200% in con-cert with the misomatic. This setting will give you at least one stop of extra latitude for after-the-fact overexposure corrections with the internal or an external RAW converter. Simply use the PUSH or PULL commands of the internal RAW converter, or move the exposure slider of your external RAW processing software.

Don't forget: ISO is just an amplification of the image signal. Using the misomatic, the amount of light that reaches the sensor is solely determined by your manual aperture and shutter speed settings. It always stays the same, regardless of the automatic ISO setting chosen by the camera. In misomatic mode, the only exposure variable is the amount of signal amplification (aka ISO), and with an ISOless sensor, this variable can also be adjusted later during RAW conversion. In this context, choosing DR200% ensures that there's ample leeway for after-the-fact exposure corrections of at least ±1 EV.

TIP 53	ISO-Bracketing: it's just a gimmick!

ISO bracketing (set the DRIVE dial to BKT and select SHOOTING SETTING > DRIVE SETTING > BKT SETTING > BKT SELECT > ISO BKT) is only available in JPEG mode, so the camera won't keep RAW files. It's just a gimmick: the camera takes a single exposure with the selected ISO setting, then creates two additional JPEGs with different ISO settings, one higher and one lower than the original setting.

ISO bracketing is just a digital push and pull operation on the intermediate RAW file (which is deleted after all three JPEGs have been generated). You could achieve the same result by shooting a single pic in FINE+RAW mode and then using the camera's built-in RAW converter to generate a second JPEG with the PULL command, and a third one with the PUSH command.

A better alternative to ISO bracketing is AE BKT. This option actually takes three different exposures and keeps the corresponding RAW files.

TIP 54	Extending the dynamic range

If the dynamic range of a subject is larger than the dynamic range of the camera's sensor and image processing, one of the following phenomena occurs:

- The highlights of the image are blown out or appear too bright (overexposed).

- Midtones appear too dark (underexposed) and shadows lose detail in the blackness.

In both cases, the shot's exposure is imbalanced. Sadly, it's very difficult (if not impossible) to restore blown highlights. It's much easier to lift underexposed midtones and blocked shadows. This procedure is called tone-mapping. Certain tonal values of the original exposure are reassigned and changed, either by employing a tone curve or by using a more complex mathematical procedure known as adaptive tone-mapping.

In order to record the full tonal range of a high-contrast subject, it's best to expose the image in a way that preserves the color and texture of the bright parts of the photo. Of course, doing so can lead to an image with underexposed midtones and blocked shadows that need further processing in order to look natural and realistic. You can correct these issues with most external RAW converters.

While every RAW converter is different, most programs offer functions to selectively change the exposure of a shot. For example, you can change the overall exposure with the exposure slider, and you can restore blown highlights with a highlight recovery slider. Most converters also offer sliders that only target shadow tones.

The DR function of the X-T2 can help you automate this tone-mapping procedure. It works in two stages:

- The RAW file is exposed one (DR200%) or two (DR400%) stops darker in order to preserve bright highlights of a scene.

- During the following RAW conversion in the camera, the underexposed shadows and midtones are digitally amplified by one (DR200%) or two (DR400%) stops to restore their natural brightness, while the (already correctly exposed) highlights are mostly left alone.

The resulting JPEG from the camera has undergone a selective exposure correction. The DR function restores the shadows and midtones of a shot that was initially exposed one or two stops darker to preserve the highlights of the scene. Looking at the resulting JPEGs, this leads to an effective gain in dynamic range (DR): one additional stop of highlight DR at DR200%, and two stops of additional highlight DR at DR400%.

In DR-Auto mode, the camera will automatically select a suitable DR setting. Please note that in this mode, the X-T2 will choose either DR100% (no highlight DR expansion) or DR200% (one stop highlight DR expansion). DR400% (two stops highlight DR expansion) is only available when it is manually selected.

You can change the DR settings of your camera in the Quick menu or by selecting IMAGE QUALITY SETTING > DYNAMIC RANGE and then either AUTO, DR100%, DR200%, or DR400%.

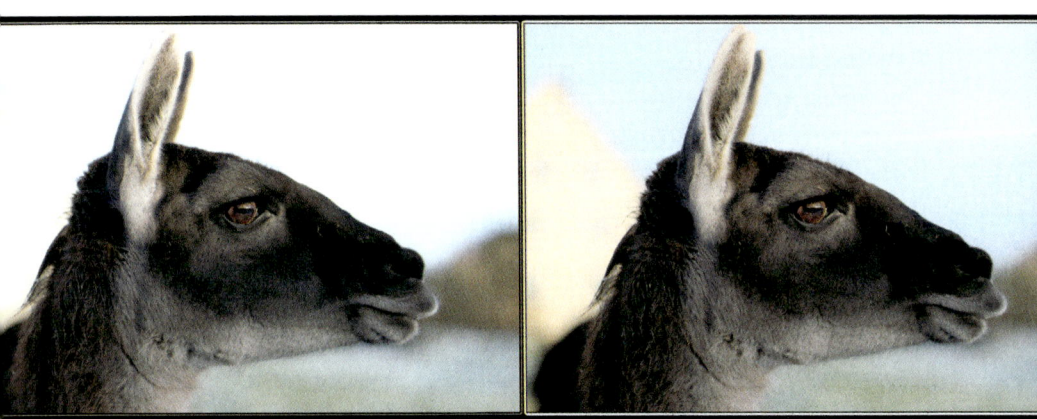

Fig. 26: These examples show the same shot with **DR100%** (left) and **DR400%** (right). At DR100%, the dark llama (our main subject) is correctly exposed, but the much brighter colors in the background are almost completely blown because they were outside of the camera's dynamic range. In the DR400% version of the shot, the exposure (brightness) of the llama didn't change. However, the bright background is now perfectly colored and textured.

Extending the dynamic range for RAW shooters	TIP 55

RAW shooters typically set the camera to DR100% and perform the tone-mapping of their shots later during RAW processing. DR100% provides a realistic live view and live histogram (WYSIWYG).

The typical strategy of a RAW shooter is to expose toward the highlights of a high-contrast scene, making sure that there's sufficient color texture in the bright parts of the shot. This can result in an image with dark midtones and blocked shadows. However, while blown highlights are hard to restore, blocked shadows can be lifted (pushed) later. Getting balanced results from scenes with a very high dynamic range can be done in almost any external RAW conversion software.

Here's what to do:

■ Use the live view and live histogram to adjust the exposure in a way that ensures that the important highlights of your scene don't blow. This will preserve the highlights, but it may also lead to darkened midtones and blocked shadows that you have to deal with later during the RAW conversion of your shot.

■ Enhance darkened shadows and midtones by selectively lifting their exposure in your RAW conversion software. For example, you could first lift the overall exposure and then restore the highlights with a highlight-recovery slider, or you could only lift the shadow tones with a shadow-tone slider. You can also combine both methods; many RAW converters are quite flexible and offer several sliders to selectively change the exposure. Lightroom and Adobe Camera RAW (ACR), for example, feature five different controls (exposure, whites, blacks, shadows, and highlights) to perform this task. Whenever you change an exposure slider, you are effectively changing the ISO of any part of the image that is affected by this slider. However, in the digital domain of the RAW conversion stage, nothing is lost and everything is fully reversible. *Selectively* changing the exposure of an image is known as tone-mapping.

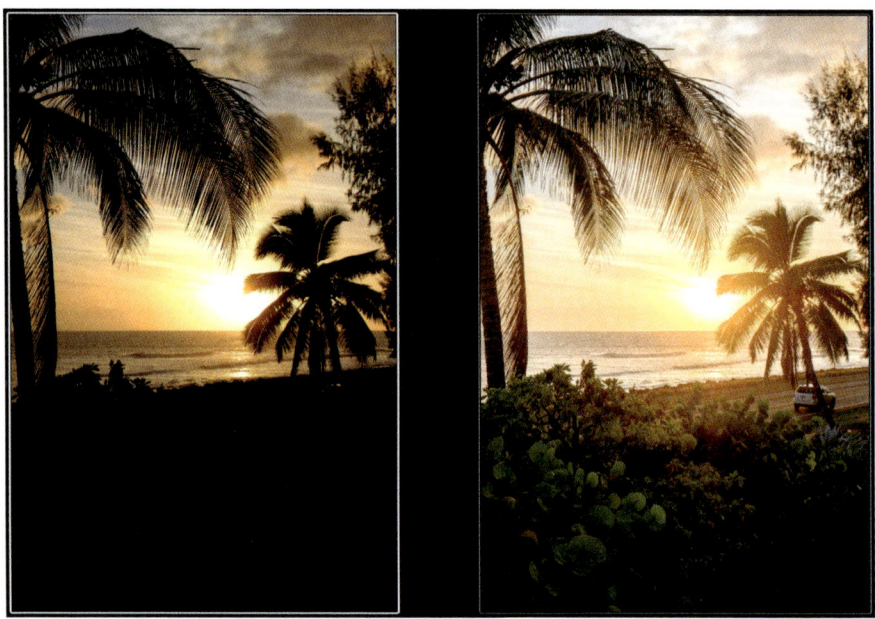

Fig. 27: The example on the left shows an image that has been exposed to the highlights. The sky is perfectly exposed, but this means that the unlit foreground is literally left in the dark. If that's what you want, great! If not, you have to apply some tone-mapping to the RAW file.

The example on the right shows the same image after some tone-mapping in Adobe Lightroom. The dark shadow regions have been lifted, revealing plenty of detail where the previous image only displayed a dark patch. This method is also known as applying adaptive ISO, because different parts of the image received a different degree of exposure push. While the shadows were pushed up (ISO increase), the highlights mostly remained as they were.

JPEG settings for RAW shooters	TIP 56

The previous tip explained the procedure to capture, compress, and later decompress scenes with high dynamic range. Since our exposure relies on the live view and the live histogram, it's useful to find camera settings that force the live histogram and live view to display as much dynamic range as possible. After all, we are shooting RAW and aren't really interested in the JPEGs from the camera, so we want the live view and live histogram to closely represent the data that will be recorded in the RAW files. This goal can be achieved by choosing JPEG parameters in the IMAGE QUALITY SETTING menu that display as much dynamic range as possible:

■ Set FILM SIMULATION to PRO NEG. STD. This setting results in JPEGs with less contrast than the other film simulation modes.

■ Set HIGHLIGHT TONE to −2. This setting reduces the highlight contrast of the JPEG—in the live view and in the live histogram.

■ Set SHADOW TONE to −2. This setting reduces the shadow contrast of the JPEG in both the live view and the live histogram.

The above JPEG settings give you a live view and live histogram with maximum dynamic range. JPEGs that are generated with these settings may look flat, but we don't care because we don't want to keep them anyway. We are only interested in the RAW file, which isn't affected by JPEG settings at all. However, the live view and live histogram are fully affected, and a flat image live view with a correspondingly flat image live histogram is exactly what we want in order to better fine-tune our exposure to preserve highlights.

You can save these JPEG settings in a custom profile (C1 to C7) so you can quickly retrieve them to set your X-T2 to RAW shooter mode. Select IMAGE QUALITY SETTING > EDIT/SAVE CUSTOM SETTING to edit your custom settings.

TIP 57	Extending the dynamic range for JPEG shooters

If you prefer to work with JPEGs from the X-T2 (or want to shoot both RAW and JPEG), you can use the camera's powerful DR function to capture scenes with high dynamic range. As you know, the DR function employs a two-stage process: reducing the exposure to capture critical highlights, and then lifting dark shadows and midtones to restore their brightness (exposure) back to realistic-looking levels.

You can simply set the camera to DR-Auto, or manually set DR200% or DR400% when you take pictures of high-contrast scenes. Remember that DR200% requires a minimum ISO setting of 400, while DR400% requires a minimum ISO setting of 800, because the shadows in your scene will eventually be amplified by one (DR200%) or two (DR400%) stops. It's best to set the camera to Auto-ISO, allowing it to pick a suitable ISO setting that corresponds with whatever DR setting you or the camera (in DR-Auto mode) may choose.

But what if we don't want to just *guess* what DR setting is optimal for any given scene? Can't we use the camera's metering to determine *exactly* how much DR expansion is required? Yes, we can!

Here's how:

- To begin with, let's set the camera to DR100% and expose toward the critical highlights of a scene, just like a RAW shooter would do. This will often require you to turn the exposure compensation dial in the negative direction until the live view and live histogram display the scene without blown highlights.

- Next, turn the exposure compensation dial in the opposite (positive) direction until the shadows and midtones are displayed as bright as you want them to appear in the final image. Here's the important part: when you turn the exposure compensation dial up again, count the number of clicks it takes to reach the target brightness of your scene. One, two, or three clicks mean you should set the camera from DR100% to DR200% for one stop of additional highlight dynamic range. More than three clicks means you should use DR400%. More than six clicks means that highlights may be blown even when you set DR400%, so you might want to avoid overcompensating beyond six clicks. As you know, each click of the exposure compensation dial equals 1/3 EV (or a third of a stop).

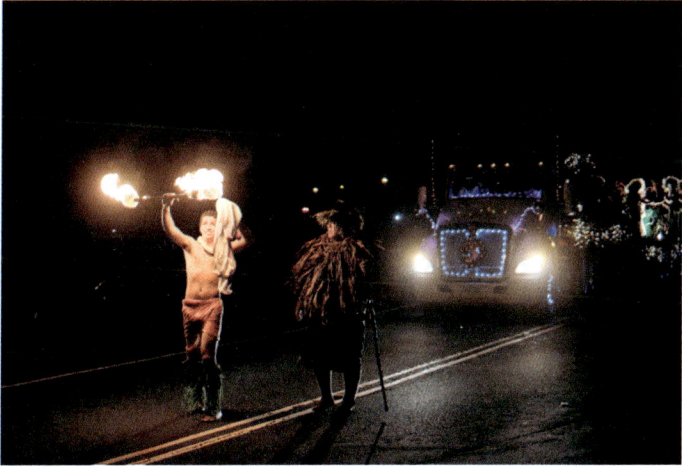

Fig. 28: **Night scenes** with bright lights and high contrast can benefit from a fixed DR400% setting in order to preserve color and texture in the highlights (Classic Chrome, DR400%).

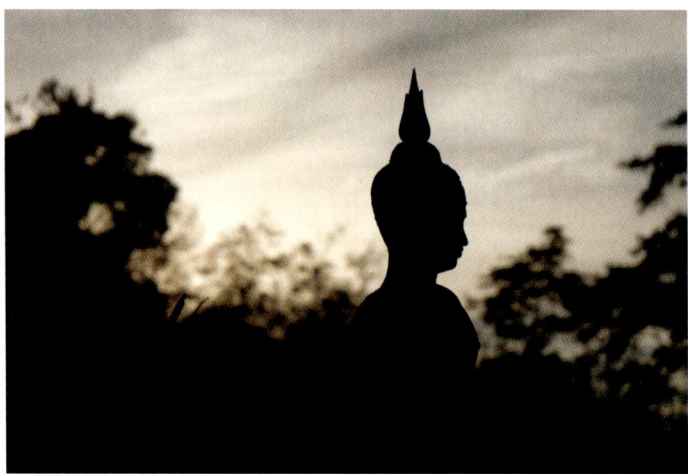

Fig. 29: On the other hand, there are instances where you may want to concentrate on the bright parts of a high-contrast scene. In such cases, a fixed DR100% setting is in order while you are exposing to the highlights (Provia, DR100%).

The two above examples illustrate that DR-Auto is not a "smart" setting; it cannot predict what the photographer has in mind. In both cases, DR-Auto would have picked DR200%—definitely not an optimal setting in either case.

*Important: The X-T2 tries to simulate the effect of manually set dynamic range expansion settings (DR200%, DR400%) in the live view and live histogram. However, automatic DR expansion via DR-Auto is **not** simulated in the live view. Instead, the live view and live histogram will show you a DR100% simulation, even when DR-Auto eventually decides to take the shot at DR200%.*

In the expanded ISO 100 setting, the live view and live histogram show the dynamic range of an ISO 200 shot, giving you the false impression of one stop more highlight dynamic range. Only when you half-press the shutter, the live view will change to display the actual dynamic range. However, in this stage, there's no live histogram available.

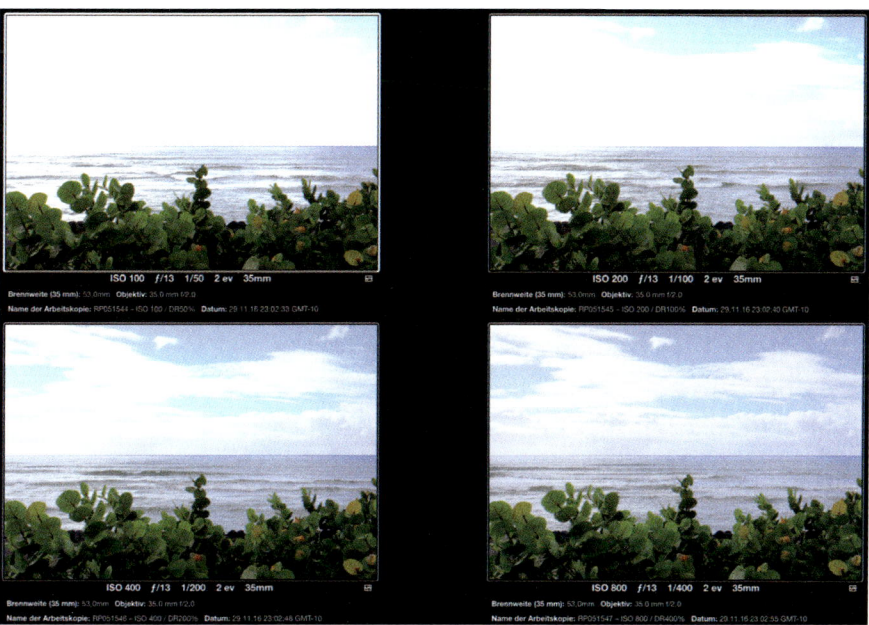

Fig. 30: **Comparing dynamic range settings:** The upper-left sample shows our scene taken with ISO 100 (aka DR50%). Highlight dynamic range is very poor; most bright parts of the image are blown.

The upper-right image shows the same scene taken with ISO 200 and DR100%. Even though there's one additional stop of highlight DR, many parts of the shot are still without structure.

On the lower left, you can see an ISO 400/DR200% version of the scene, which is giving us another stop of highlight dynamic range. In this example, the clouds and the sky are already looking much better.

The lower-right example is an ISO 800/DR400% version of our scene, which has two added stops of highlight dynamic range compared to a standard ISO 200/DR100% shot. Here, everything is smooth and shiny, with plenty of texture in the clouds and no discoloration of the sky.

Using the DR function for high-key and portrait photography	TIP 58

High-key photography [40] delivers images with tones that mostly occupy the right half of the histogram. High-key images can be achieved by lighting a scene brightly and uniformly with little differences in contrast, and then overexposing the scene by one or two stops. This results in images with a bright, clean, and joyful look. This is why high-key is often used for product shots, portraits, and advertising.

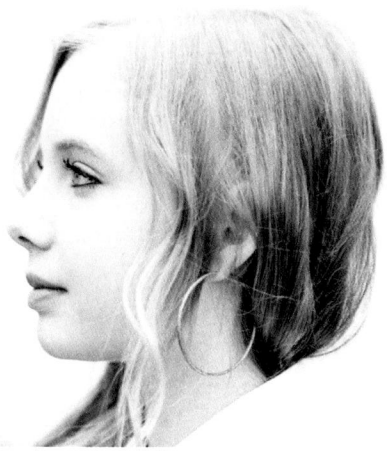

Fig. 31: I took this **high-key sample** under an overcast sky with soft, uniform natural lighting. I placed the model in front of a bright wall. Thanks to the resulting low contrast, the scene could be shot with a bright exposure at ISO 200 and DR100% without blowing critical highlights.

Normally, high-key photographs require suitable low-contrast lighting. If the contrast is too big, a bright exposure of the darker tones would lead to blown highlights.

To be suitable for high-key, most of your scene has to fit into the right half of the histogram. If that's not the case, there are two options: you can either reduce the contrast of the scene by applying fill light (like installing a flash setup), or you can apply appropriate tone-mapping (pushing the shadows and midtones while protecting the highlights) during RAW conversion.

Thanks to the DR function, the second option is also available in-camera. This means that you can generate JPEGs with a high-key look directly in your X-T2.

Here's how:

- Set the camera to manual exposure mode M and turn off Auto-ISO, so aperture, shutter speed, and ISO can be set manually. Make sure to set the dynamic range to DR100%.

- Expose the scene as usual to protect critical highlights that you do not want to blow. The live view and live histogram are your friends. Set aperture, shutter speed, and ISO accordingly. Take a test shot to be sure that the scene is exposed as brightly as possible without any blown critical highlights.

- Now double your ISO setting (for example, from ISO 200 to ISO 400) and change the dynamic range setting from DR100% to DR200%. Don't change your aperture and shutter speed, though!

- In the live view and live histogram, your scene will be looking brighter. Take another shot with these new settings and inspect the resulting high-key JPEG in your camera's playback mode.

As far as the RAW data is concerned, it makes no difference whether you shoot the same scene with ISO 200, DR100%, f/5.6, and 1/1000s, or with ISO 400, DR200%, f/5.6, and 1/1000s. Even ISO 800, DR400%, f/5.6, and 1/1000s would result in exactly the same RAW data all over again. However, you will see a huge difference in the corresponding straight-out-of-camera JPEGs: shadows and midtones will appear increasingly bright (high-key), but the brightest highlights will be protected: this is the X-T2's built-in tone-mapping at work.

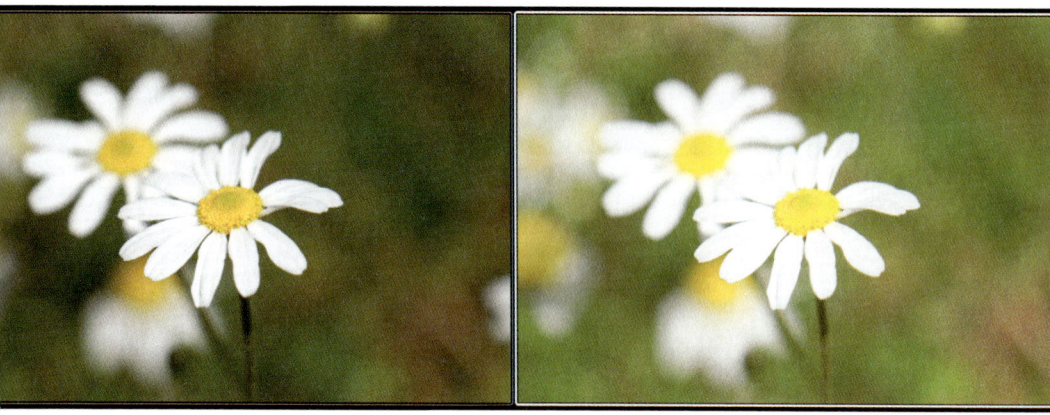

Fig. 32: **Turning the DR function into a virtual high-key studio:** The example on the left illustrates a regular exposure of a flower at ISO 200, DR100%, f/5.6, and 1/1000s. The exposure was designed to protect the structure of the white petals. The example on the right is the same scene shot at ISO 400, DR200%, f/5.6, and 1/1000s. This means that while the RAW data remains the same, only the JPEG from the ISO 400/DR200% version delivers the desired high-key look while leaving the structure of the petals intact. Doubling ISO and DR settings in tandem (leaving all other exposure parameters untouched) moves the histogram of the shot to the right, but without blowing bright highlights. Instead of cutting them off, the tonality of the bright highlights is compressed. You can fine-tune such results with the camera's built-in RAW converter, for example, by reducing the highlight contrast (HIGHLIGHT TONE settings). Additionally, you can revert a high-key shot that was taken (for example) at ISO 400/DR200% into a regular ISO 200/DR100% JPEG by reprocessing the RAW image in the built-in RAW converter using PULL −1 EV and DR100% settings.

Tone-mapping and tonality compression can also be used to improve portraits. It can reduce contrast and harsh shadows on faces that are illuminated by a single light source, such as the sun. With our high-key technique, dark eyes and shadows under the nose can be lifted without blowing the bright parts of the skin. At the same time, the tone-mapping and highlight tone compression makes skin blemishes almost disappear.

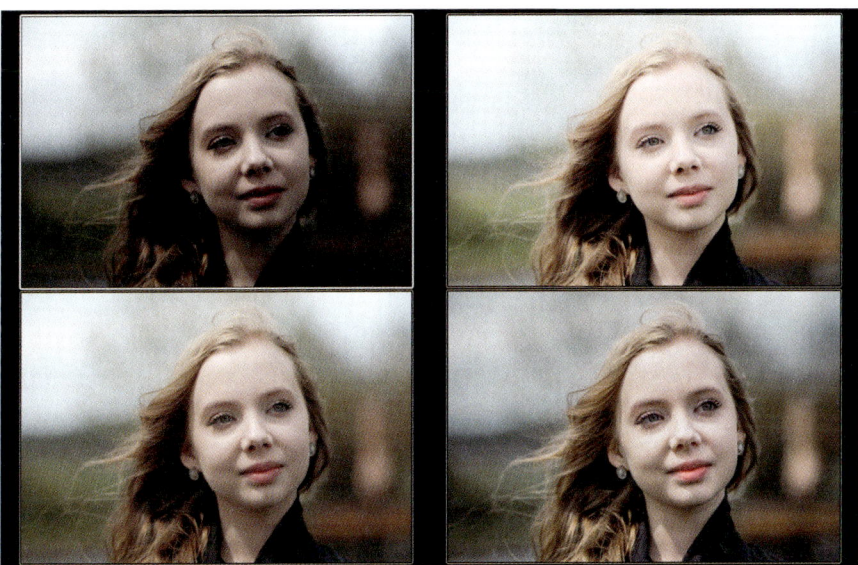

Fig. 33: **Using virtual high-key in a portrait:** This example illustrates a difficult portrait situation with strong contrast and harsh shadows on the face.

The upper-left sample shows a JPEG that was created by exposing for the highlights with the CLASSIC CHROME film simulation and ISO 200. This resulted in a rather dark face with strong contrast and shadows.

The upper-right image shows the same shot two stops brighter, and with extended highlight dynamic range to protect the highlights. This means using ISO 800 and DR400% while maintaining the exposure (aperture and shutter speed) of the upper-left sample. Additionally, I set HIGHLIGHT TONE to −2 to pull back the brightest (skin) tones. As you can see, the eyes are now much brighter and the harsh contrasts are gone.

Too much? Don't worry! Using the X-T2's built-in RAW converter, you can always create more realistic versions of your high-key shots. In this case (lower-left image), I used PULL −1 (effectively pulling the shot from ISO 800 down to ISO 400) along with DR200% (to compensate for the pull), SHADOW TONE −2 (for more shadow detail), and HIGHLIGHT TONE −1 (to bring back the brightest skin tones).

Alternatively, you can also process the RAW file in any external RAW converter. In the case of the lower-right example, I used Adobe Lightroom.

Creating **HDR images** with the X-T2

A popular method of capturing high-contrast scenes is HDR photography. HDR [41] means High Dynamic Range: multiple images of the scene are taken at different exposure levels and then merged into a single image with extended dynamic range. The latter can be facilitated with specialized software, such as HDR Efex Pro by NIK/Google or Photomatix Pro by HDRsoft.

Typically, HDR requires a minimum of two different exposures of a scene, but some photographers don't stop there. They take five, seven, or even nine different exposures, each separated from the other by (usually) one stop or EV (exposure value).

Here's a procedure that you can use to quickly generate nine different exposures of a scene:

- Put the X-T2 on a tripod or a similar device. If your lens features an OIS, make sure to turn it off.

- Connect a remote shutter release or set the self-timer to 2 seconds to avoid camera shake.

- Set the camera to aperture priority **A**.

- Choose a low ISO setting (such as 200). Don't use ISO 100, though!

- Deactivate any DR expansion by setting the dynamic range to DR100%.

- Select a suitable aperture for your shot and scene and use manual focus. This ensures that all nine images will be focused exactly the same. If you like, you can also use adapted manual focus lenses.

- Set the DRIVE dial to BKT and select AE BKT with a variation of ±1 in the SHOOTING SETTING > DRIVE SETTING > BKT SETTING menu to activate the camera's auto exposure bracketing.

- Select AVERAGE exposure metering.

Having prepared the camera for HDR, you can now follow these steps to capture the actual images:

- Set the exposure compensation dial to neutral (0) and press the shutter release. Make sure to either use a remote shutter release or the self-timer. The camera will now record the first three shots of the scene, with exposure levels of 0 EV, −1 EV, and +1 EV.

- Set the exposure compensation dial to −3 EV and press the shutter release. The camera is now recording three more images that deviate −4 EV, −3 EV, and −2 EV from the original exposure.

- Finally, set the exposure compensation dial to +3 EV. After releasing the shutter, you'll get three more exposures, this time with +2 EV, +3 EV, and +4 EV.

This procedure results in nine different exposures that you can merge using the HDR software of your choice that will result in an image with an additional dynamic range of ±4 EV.

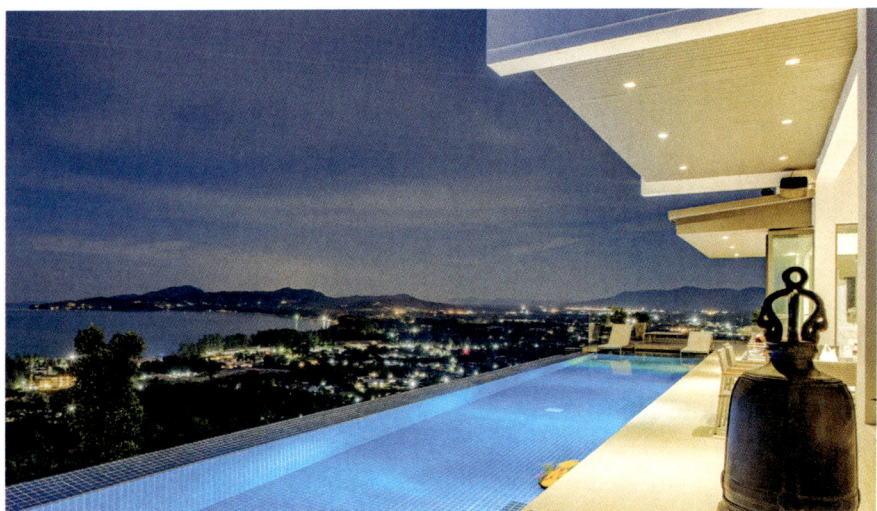

Fig. 34: This **HDR image** consists of two RAW shots that were taken with an exposure difference of 5 EV and merged in Adobe Lightroom.

Please note that the slowest shutter speed in all AE modes is 30 seconds, so your basic exposure (with 0 EV correction) should not be longer than 2 seconds. If you require shots that exceed 30 seconds of exposure time, it's better to use manual mode **M** in concert with the Bulb (B) setting of the shutter speed dial.

TIP 60	HDR: the handheld way

Thanks to the ISOless sensor in the X-T2, you can effectively take handheld HDR shots by combining two vastly differently exposed RAW files to one HDR-DNG file in Adobe Lightroom or Adobe Camera RAW.

Let's start with how to prepare the camera for this endeavor:

- Set the X-T2 to aperture priority **A**.

- Select a low ISO setting, such as ISO 200. Don't set ISO 100.

- Make sure the dynamic range is set to DR100%.

- Pre-select a suitable aperture.

- Set BKT on the DRIVE dial and select AE BKT with a variation of ±2 in the SHOOTING SETTING > DRIVE SETTING > BKT SETTING menu to activate the camera's auto exposure bracketing.

- Select AVERAGE exposure metering.

- Use the "JPEG settings for RAW shooters" setup: FILM SIMULATION > PRO NEG. STD, SHADOW TONE −2 and HIGHLIGHT TONE −2.

- Select SET UP > BUTTON/DIAL SETTING > AE/AF-LOCK MODE > AE&AF ON/OFF SWITCH.

Now let's take our HDR shots:

- Expose to the highlights! Using the live view and live histogram, frame your scene, and turn the exposure compensation dial until critical highlights aren't blown. When you are finished, memorize the shutter speed that is displayed.

- Save the exposure from the previous step by pressing the AE-L button, but do so without changing the framing of your shot. Make sure that the locked exposure has the same shutter speed as the one from the previous step.

- Now correct the exposure by +2 EV using the exposure compensation dial: simply turn it six clicks in the plus direction. This will shift your locked exposure up by two stops.

- Focus and press the shutter button to take the shot. Hold the camera very steady while the X-T2 takes a quick burst of three consecutive AE bracketing shots (each with a different exposure). We are only interested in the last two of these three shots because their exposure differs by 4 EV.

- Import the RAW files of the last two of the three bracketing shots into Adobe Lightroom or Adobe Camera RAW, where you can merge them into a single HDR-DNG file using the HDR function. You can process the HDR-DNG file in Lightroom like any normal RAW file.

This trick combines several functions and techniques that were discussed in previous tips, such as AE bracketing, exposure compensation, and AE-Lock. By combining two shots with the significant exposure difference of 4 EV, we dramatically enhance the overall dynamic range of the image. Since the two shots in question were taken in a quick burst with maximum continuous drive speed, there's also little or no motion blur in the resulting DNG composite. This trick can even work for (slowly) moving subjects, especially since Lightroom's HDR merge tool includes automatic de-ghosting.

The darker of the two shots is perfectly exposed to the highlights, while the brighter shot brings 4 EV less shot noise to the table. Since our ISOless X-T2 provides very little sensor read noise, we can easily push the brighter RAW partition up another 3 EV without sacrificing image quality. This adds up to a whopping 7 EV of *additional* dynamic range, which should be enough to overcome every dynamic range challenge you may encounter in your photographic life. Even better, you can use this process for handheld shots—as long as the shutter speed of the brighter shot is fast enough to prevent blurriness caused by camera shake.

TIP 61	Using the electronic shutter

The electronic shutter (ES) of the X-T2 offers three major advantages: it is completely silent, it eliminates vibrations from shutter shock, and it allows shutter speeds as fast as 1/32000s. That's great in situations where you want to be particularly stealthy, or when you want to use fast lenses (like the XF56mmF1.2 R) with wide-open aperture in bright light and spare yourself the hassle of attaching an ND filter.

You can set which shutter type the camera is supposed to use in SHOOTING SETTING > SHUTTER TYPE. There are three available options:

- **MS:** The camera is only using the mechanical shutter. This is the default setting and also my recommended standard setting.

- **ES:** This setting switches the X-T2 to its electronic shutter with available shutter speeds between 30s and 1/32000s, and ISO settings between 200 and 12800. You cannot fire a flash when the ES is in use.

- **MS+ES:** In this mode, the camera combines both shutter types. It will automatically use the ES for shutter speeds faster than 1/8000s. Flash photography is only possible within the envelope of the mechanical shutter.

To set shutter speeds faster than 1/8000s, select 1/8000s with the shutter speed dial, then turn the command dial to the right. Alternatively, you can set the shutter speed dial to **T** and access all available shutter speeds with the command dial in 1/3 EV steps.

Please note that even at 1/32000s, the electronic shutter needs about 1/20s to capture all image contents. In other words, it takes the electronic shutter 1/20s to record all 24 megapixels of the sensor. This effect, known as Rolling Shutter [42], can lead to weird distortions when you are taking pictures of fast-moving subjects. In addition, image quality can deteriorate when the ES is used in concert with pulsing or flickering artificial light sources. The long read-out time and the rolling shutter are also responsible for the restrictions regarding flash photography.

Since the electronic shutter is completely silent, the camera is generating an artificial shutter sound when the ES is in use. The nature and volume of this sound effect can be set in SET UP > SOUND SET-UP, where you can also switch it off entirely.

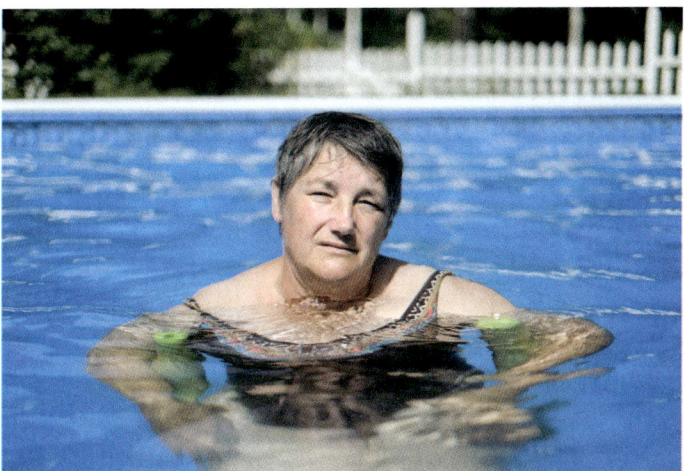

Fig. 35: The **electronic shutter** is a practical option for shots taken with fast lenses in bright light, when 1/8000s simply isn't fast enough to avoid overexposure.

2.4 FOCUSING WITH THE X-T2

The X-T2 features a hybrid autofocus system that combines CDAF and PDAF. CDAF, PDAF, hybrid AF? It can be quite confusing.

- CDAF means **C**ontrast **D**etection **A**uto**F**ocus and is the current standard in mirrorless cameras. CDAF is available throughout the entire sensor area (91 or 325 AF frames in Single Point mode or 91 AF frames in Zone and Wide/Tracking mode). It works quite precisely, but is not particularly fast.

- PDAF means **P**hase **D**etection **A**uto**F**ocus and is the current standard in DSLRs. Since the X-T2 is mirrorless, its PDAF works directly on the sensor, but is only available throughout the 49 (respectively 169) central AF frames. PDAF is pretty fast and particularly good at tracking moving subjects. It can predict where a moving object will be a split second from now, a feature that can be quite useful when you shoot in burst mode.

- **Hybrid AF** means that the X-T2 automatically chooses the best method (CDAF or PDAF) for the current subject and the current light conditions.

TIP 62	**CDAF and PDAF:** what's the difference?

Both AF methods offer distinct qualities that can be useful during your daily shooting:

- CDAF focuses on surfaces and works best with areas that offer a lot of contrast. A solid white or black wall doesn't work well with CDAF, but a checkered wall works great. It's the same with clothes: unicolor may not work, but patterned clothes work wonderfully. CDAF operates with a trial-and-error approach: it keeps adjusting the focus until it finds the distance setting with the utmost contrast. CDAF doesn't directly go to the optimal focus setting. This results in heightened autofocus motor activity and visible focus hunting while the AF goes back and forth until it finds the optimal focus position.

- PDAF in the X-T2 loves focusing on edges, especially vertical edges (or horizontal ones if you hold the camera upright). Unlike CDAF, PDAF is able to directly determine the distance to an object, so there's no need for focus hunting. That's why PDAF is considerably faster.

- Both methods depend on good light to work with maximum efficiency. The brighter a scene is and the more contrast it has, the better the AF will work. Bright lenses with large maximum aperture openings are beneficial because they allow the AF to work with more light and less depth of field, which helps increase the precision of the CDAF. It's worth noting that most lenses are less bright near their edges than they are at the center (this effect is called vignetting), so in bad lighting, the autofocus may work less efficiently with AF frames that are located far off center.

AF-S or AF-C?	TIP 63

Your X-T2 features two basic AF modes that can be selected with the focus selector at the front of the camera:

- **AF-S (AF Single) is meant for stationary subjects**. Once you half-press the shutter button, the camera will focus on the object covered by the active AF frame and lock the distance (as long as you keep the shutter button half-depressed). You can either fully press the shutter button to take the shot, or you can take your finger off the shutter release and try again.

- **AF-C (AF Continuous) is meant for moving subjects,** especially those that move toward or away from the camera. When you half-press the shutter button, the camera starts focusing on the object covered by the active AF frame and continuously adjusts the distance to the moving object as long as you keep the shutter button half-depressed. In the live view, this may look like the camera is continuously hunting, while the green AF confirmation dot in the bottom-left corner of the screen keeps going on and off. Don't worry! This is normal: the hybrid AF (PDAF and CDAF) has a pretty good track record of getting the moving object in focus when the shutter button is finally fully depressed. Just make sure that the active AF frame or AF zone always covers the part of the image that is supposed to be in focus. Don't forget that PDAF (with its predictive tracking capability) is only available in concert with one of the central AF frames.

- Every camera experiences a small delay between pressing the shutter and actually recording the image. This shutter lag can be taken into account by the predictive PDAF: the camera isn't focusing on the object's current position, but on the position the object is *predicted* to be when the image is actually captured. Please note that predictive autofocus is also possible with CDAF, though to a lesser degree of performance.

- While AF-C focuses using the set working aperture, AF-S can open up the aperture beyond working aperture to improve the AF performance in poor light. This also improves focusing accuracy due to the reduced depth of field caused by the wide open aperture.

TIP 64   AF modes: **Single Point AF vs. Zone AF vs. Wide/Tracking AF**

In AF/MF SETTING > AF MODE (or in the Quick menu) you can choose between SINGLE POINT, ZONE, or WIDE/TRACKING autofocus:

■ **Single Point AF** mode is my recommended AF setting for most applications. In this mode, you have to manually select one of 91 (or 325) available AF frames. Try to avoid old habits like using only the central frame in concert with the focus and recompose [43] technique. It's better to compose the shot and *then* select a suitable AF frame that covers the part of the image that needs to be in perfect focus. This helps you avoid focus errors that invariably occur when you pan the focus plane in another direction. Such focus errors may be irrelevant with long focal lengths and small aperture openings (large depth of field), but they can be quite unpleasant with wide-angle lenses, a wide aperture opening (small DOF), and situations with a short distance between the camera and the subject. Single Point AF can be used in concert with both AF-S and AF-C.

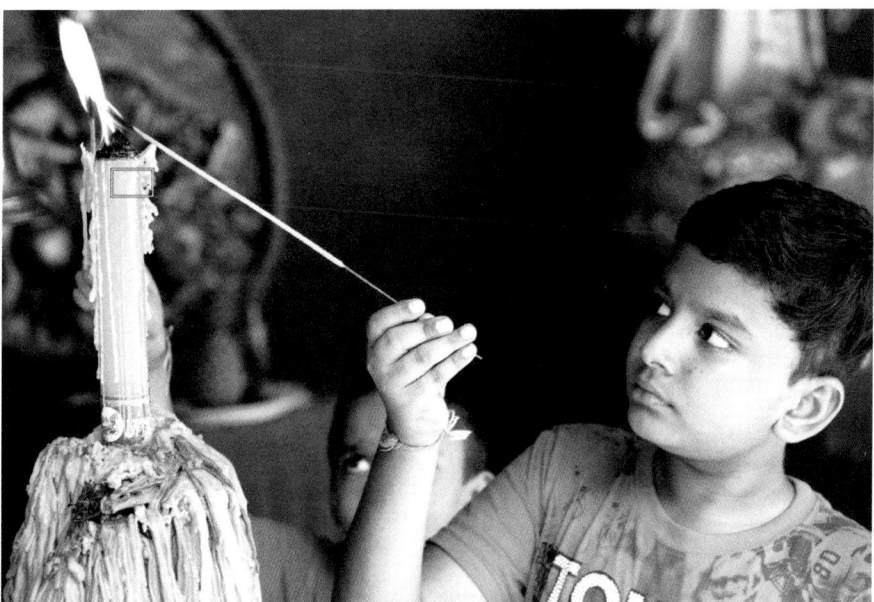

Fig. 36: Shooting with **minimal depth of field,** you can't afford to use a focus and recompose habit because it would quickly lead to soft results that appear out of focus. Instead, compose the shot, and then focus using a single autofocus frame (there are 91 or 325 to choose from in Single Point AF mode) that covers the part of the image that is supposed to be in focus.

- You can think of **Zone AF** as an extension of Single Point AF. Basically, an AF zone is a particularly large AF frame that consists of a set of smaller AF points. Zones are available in sizes that cover 3×3, 5×5, or 7×7 out of a total of 91 AF points. Like Single Point AF frames, AF zones can be moved around within the image area. Since they are larger, AF zones make it easier to focus on moving subjects. In Zone AF mode, the camera will start looking for something to focus on in the center (crosshairs) of the selected zone and then expand its search toward the edges of the zone until it finds a target. Like Single Point AF, Zone AF works in concert with either AF-S or AF-C.

- When you combine **Wide/Tracking AF** mode with **AF-S**, the camera scans the entire image frame and automatically selects up to 9 out of 91 available AF frames. It's a bit like rolling dice, since the camera is looking for areas with a lot of contrast. It doesn't know what's important in a scene. This changes when Wide/Tracking is used in concert with **AF-C:** This combination offers real 3D tracking of moving objects; that is, objects that not only move toward or away from the camera, but also left, right, up, or down within the image frame. In order to track such an object, select Wide/Tracking and AF-C and pick one of the 91 available AF points. To start the tracking process, make sure the selected point covers the moving object you want to track. Half-press the shutter button to start the tracking process. As long as you keep the shutter-button half-pressed, the camera will automatically follow the selected subject with a cloud of small AF frames as it moves across the image area.

Please note that Fujifilm has released an *AF Special Website* detailing the autofocus modes and mode combinations that come with your X-T2. You can access it by clicking here [44].

In addition to that, I have published a blog article describing the new AF features that came with firmware 4 for the X-T1. These features are also found in the X-T2. Click here [45] to read it. This article also contains links to short videos with examples of Single Point AF, Zone AF, and Wide/Tracking AF.

Selecting an AF frame or AF zone	TIP 65

The X-T2 offers an indirect and a direct method for selecting one of its 91 or 325 available AF frames in Single Point AF and for moving an AF zone around in Zone AF:

The *indirect* method requires you to *first* press the AF button and *then* use the selector buttons to pick an AF frame or move an AF zone. Since the X-T2 doesn't feature a hard-wired AF button, you have to assign this function to one of the Fn buttons by pressing and holding the desired Fn button until its configuration menu appears. Then you can select FOCUS AREA.

The *direct* method involves using the focus stick to move the focus frame or focus zone in eight different directions. Pressing the focus stick has the same effect as pressing the AF button. For all this to work as expected, the FOCUS LEVER SETTING needs to be set to ON. This setting can be reached by pressing and holding the focus stick until the configuration menu appears.

Choosing a suitable **AF frame or AF zone size**	TIP 66

The X-T2 offers 91 (or 325) different AF frames in Single Point AF, and each frame comes in five different sizes. You can change the size of an AF frame by pressing the AF button (or the focus stick) and turning one of the command dials left or right to decrease or increase the frame size.

AF frame size affects the efficiency of CDAF and PDAF. A basic rule to follow is: *Make your AF frame as large as possible and as small as necessary.*

This is why:

- With a large AF frame size, the camera has more to work with and a better chance to find contrast, especially when the light conditions aren't optimal. There's also a higher chance the camera will be able to use the faster PDAF method when one of the central AF frames is active. When PDAF isn't available, the camera will fall back to the slower CDAF.

- With a smaller AF frame size, the autofocus becomes more accurate. A small AF frame gives you better control over what *exactly* the camera is focusing on. Avoid AF frame sizes that are larger than the part of your image that needs to be in focus. For example, if your AF frame is larger than the head of the person you are focusing on, there's a chance that the camera will instead focus on the background behind them, especially if that background contains a lot of contrast.

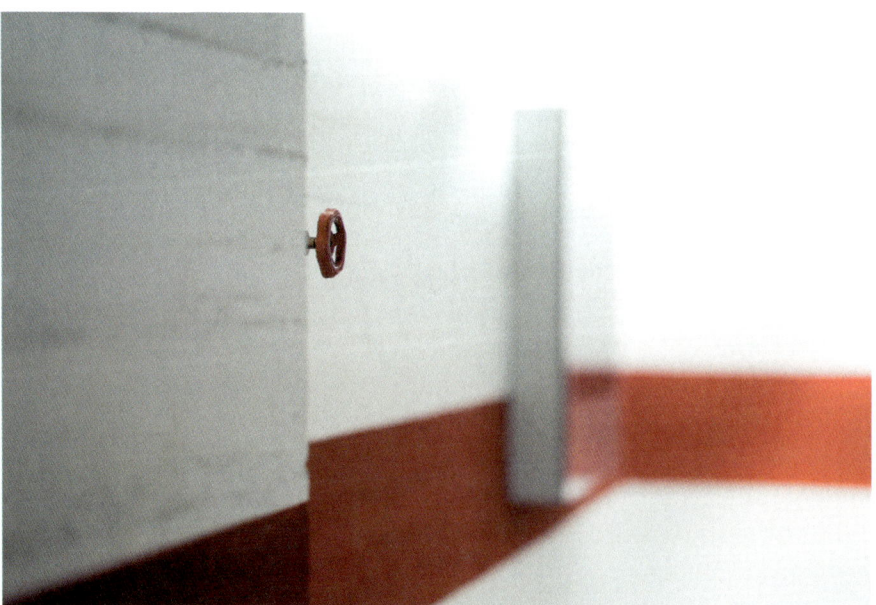

Fig. 37: To get tiny parts of an image in perfect focus, it's best to choose a small AF frame size.

In a similar fashion, you can change the size of AF zones by pressing the AF button (or the focus stick) and turning the command dial left or right. You have a choice of three AF zone sizes: 3×3 (default), 5×5, or 7×7 out of 91 frames.

Since we can regard AF zones as very large AF frames, the same rules apply: larger zones are more convenient, and they potentially offer a faster AF response; but they are also potentially less accurate than smaller zones.

Keep in mind that the faster PDAF method is only available if the zone doesn't extend beyond the central PDAF point matrix. As soon as an AF zone is configured to include at least one CDAF-only AF point, the focus system will switch to CDAF. You can tell the difference between AF points that are PDAF-enabled and those that are CDAF-only because the 49 (or 169) PDAF-enabled points are displayed as larger squares than the surrounding CDAF-only points.

Manual focus and DOF zone focusing	TIP 67

To set the camera to manual focus, move the focus selector at the front of your X-T2 to the **M** position. There are several manual focus aids available:

- A magnification tool with two magnification levels

- Focus peaking (Focus Peak Highlight) with two strength levels and optional colors (red or blue)

- Digital split image

- An electronic distance scale with depth-of-field bars that can be based on two formats: PIXEL BASIS and FILM FORMAT BASIS

- One-Touch-AF (or Instant AF): autofocus in MF with the AF-L button

The digital distance scale can help you define a focus zone with pre-determined depth of field (DOF). As long as you opt for PIXEL BASE in AF/MF SETTING > DEPTH-OF-FIELD SCALE, everything within the DOF zone will look pixel-sharp even when the image is magnified to a 100% view. Please don't confuse manual zone focusing with Zone AF—they are completely different.

Here's a zone-focusing example: using an 18mm lens, manually set a distance of 15 feet and stop down to f/6.4. The DOF bars will show a depth-of-field zone that begins at around 12 feet and ends at around 30 feet. This means that everything located in this zone (between 12 and 30 feet) will appear equally in focus in the final image. All you have to do is make sure that your subject is within that zone when you press the shutter button.

A special case of manual zone focusing is setting the hyperfocal distance [46]. This is the distance setting with the maximum DOF (all the way to infinity). Again, the electronic DOF scale can be very helpful: all you have to do is manually set the distance where the blue DOF bar on the right touches the infinity mark. For example, using an 18mm lens at f/16, the hyperfocal distance is at about 16 feet, with the pixel-sharp DOF zone extending from nine feet to infinity.

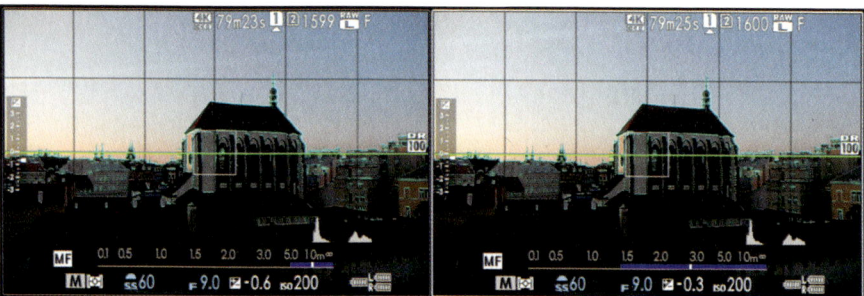

Fig. 38: Setting the **hyperfocal distance** with the electronic distance and DOF scale: instead of focusing on a predetermined distance, manually change the focus distance until the blue DOF bar touches the infinity mark on the right end of the scale. This gives us the hyperfocal distance for a given aperture and focal length. This image shows the hyperfocal distance of a wide-angle lens at f/9 for both the PIXEL BASIS format (left) and FILM FORMAT BASIS format (right).

Please note that depth of field is very much dependent on the circle of confusion [13] (CoC). Fujifilm uses a very conservative CoC that guarantees pixel-sharp results even when the DOF zone is viewed at 100% magnification on a computer screen. Fuji is literally using the sensor's maximum resolution as a benchmark. In PIXEL BASIS mode, everything that's located within the electronic DOF zone will be rendered at least as sharp as the sensor can resolve it. In the age of pixel peeping, this is as good as it can get.

It's important to know that the engraved analog distance and DOF scales on the XF14mmF2.8, XF16mmF1.4, and XF23mmF1.4 lenses follow a different rule: the FILM FORMAT BASIS option. They are based on a less conservative circle of confusion that is several aperture stops more generous than the electronic PIXEL BASIS scale. You can change the electronic scale to FILM FORMAT BASIS (and hence use a less conservative scale with all your lenses) in the AF/MF SETTING > DEPTH-OF-FIELD SCALE menu.

Manual focus assistants: focus peaking and digital split image	TIP 68

The X-T2 features two MF assistants:

- **Focus Peaking** (or Focus Peak Highlight) emphasizes the edges of objects when they are in focus. This method is especially useful in concert with longer focal lengths and bright lenses with a tiny DOF.

- **Digital Split Image** tries to simulate the split image indicator of analog SLRs. It works best with vertical lines (or horizontal lines when the camera is held in portrait orientation). It uses the sensor's PDAF-enabled area, which is why the digital split image is just as large as the area covered by the central PDAF frames.

To quickly switch between the two MF assistants, you can press and hold the rear command dial for about a second while you are in MF mode.

You can watch a short video demonstrating the manual focus assistants here [47].

TIP 69	Focus check: use the **magnifier tool!**

The magnifier tool is helpful for checking whether or not the current focus is spot-on. Simply press the rear command dial (either in AF-S/Single Point AF or in MF mode) to magnify everything that is covered by the active focus frame.

You can change the magnification level by turning the rear command dial. You can also combine the focus check with both MF assistants (focus peaking and digital split image). Please note that in digital split image mode, there's only *one* magnification level available.

By selecting AF/MF SETTING > FOCUS CHECK > ON, the magnifier tool is *automatically* activated when you turn the manual focus ring of a lens in MF mode. You can immediately cancel any automatic focus check by half-pressing the shutter button.

Similar to the AF-S and AF-C modes, there are 91 (or 325) different MF frames in manual focus mode. These frames indicate which part of the image will be magnified when focus check is activated. As usual, you can change the active frame by pressing the AF button or focus stick, and then moving the MF frame around with the selector keys or the stick.

TIP 70	One-Touch-AF (Instant AF)

One-Touch-AF (or Instant AF) allows you to use autofocus in manual focus mode. All you have to do is press the AF-L button. One-Touch-AF always works with a wide-open aperture and works with both PDAF and CDAF. Like normal autofocus, its efficiency depends on the size of the selected focus frame.

One-Touch-AF is the most precise AF method available, which also makes it a bit slower than the camera's normal autofocus. It can be combined with conventional manual focusing: you can use One-Touch-AF to quickly autofocus on an object, then manually fine-tune the focus by turning the focus ring and using MF assistants like the magnifier and focus peaking. Please note that this convenient method of fine-tuning One-Touch-AF with manual focus is *not* available when you are using lenses with manual focus clutches (XF14mmF2.8, XF16mmF1.4, and XF23mmF1.4).

One-Touch-AF normally works like AF-S, but you can also set it to continuous focus with AF/MF SETTING > INSTANT AF SETTING > AF-C. In this mode, One-Touch-AF will track an object as long as you keep the AF-L button depressed in manual focus mode. Unlike normal AF-C, One-Touch-AF-C can focus with a wide-open aperture (instead of the set working aperture) when the light is poor, making it an option for stage and concert photography with moving subjects. Just keep the AF-L button depressed for continuous instant autofocus as you press the shutter button in the right moment.

Using **AF+MF**	TIP 71

AF+MF enables you to focus in AF mode, then adjust the focus manually by turning the focus ring, all while holding the shutter button half-depressed. Select AF/MF SETTING > AF+MF > ON to enable this feature. In order to use AF+MF, your X-T2 has to be in AF-S autofocus mode.

Here's how it works:

- Autofocus on your subject as usual in AF-S mode by half-pressing the shutter button.

- Once the autofocus has been confirmed (green square[s]) or not confirmed (red AF warning), keep the shutter button half-depressed and rotate the focus ring of your lens to *manually* adjust the focus distance until you are satisfied. If Focus Peaking is enabled, it will automatically engage as soon as the focus ring is rotated and manual focus (MF) kicks in. You can also use the Focus Check function (AF/MF SETTING > FOCUS CHECK > ON) to automatically magnify the focus area as soon as you turn the focus ring. For this to work, make sure that AF-S and SINGLE POINT AF are set. You can also combine Focus Check magnification with Focus Peaking. Turn the rear command dial to change the magnification factor and press the rear command dial to manually enable/disable the live view magnification. Remember that all this needs to be performed while you keep the shutter button half-depressed, so this might need some practice.

■ When you are happy with your manual focus adjustments, fully depress the half-pressed shutter button to take the shot.

I see three main applications for AF+MF:

■ **Manual focus in situations when autofocus fails:** Instead of losing time by changing the focus mode from AF to MF, you can immediately focus manually when the camera's AF fails to acquire the subject. Simply adjust the focus manually using the focus ring.

■ **Correcting the camera's autofocus:** There are instances when you might want to fine-tune the autofocus of your camera by adjusting it manually. Again, Focus Peaking is available to make things easier, and you can enable Focus Check to automatically show a magnified view of the focus area when you turn the focus ring.

■ **Shifting the depth-of-field (DOF) zone or setting the hyperfocal distance:** After half-pressing the shutter button, AF+MF lets you quickly shift the DOF zone toward or away from the camera by turning the focus ring. The digital distance scale on the screen can be quite helpful here. For example, you can shift the right tip of the blue DOF bar to just touch the infinity mark of the digital distance scale to set the hyperfocal distance [48].

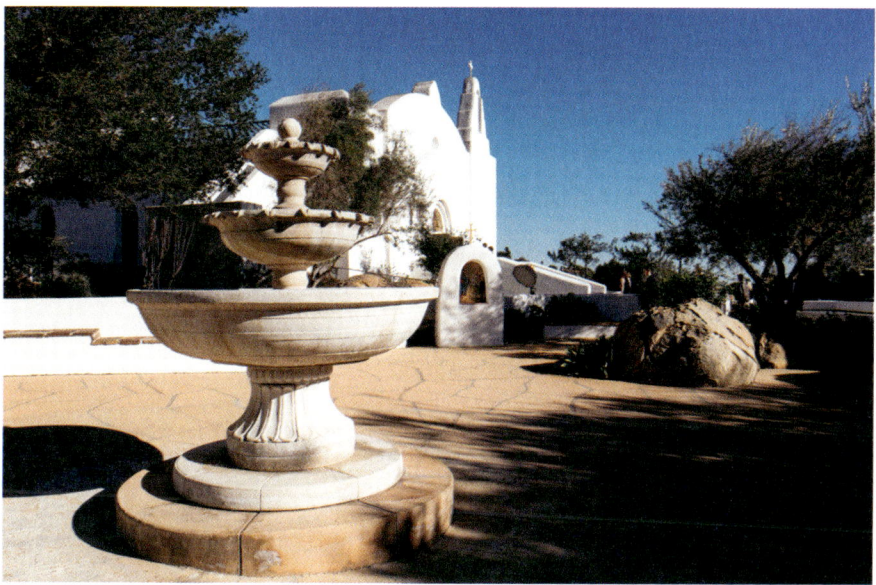

Fig. 39: In the example above, I autofocused on the fountain by placing the AF frame right over it. I used a small aperture of f/16 for plenty of depth of field (DOF). Since the portion of the DOF zone that extends in front of the fountain toward the camera is useless in this case, I manually shifted the DOF zone away from the camera using **AF+MF.** The resulting DOF zone starts at the fountain and extends all the way back.

At first glance, the MF component of AF+MF may look like your usual manual focus, but it's not. While genuine MF is always performed at wide-open aperture, the MF part of AF+MF is performed at the selected working aperture. That's because the shutter button is half-pressed, so the camera has already been primed to take the shot with minimal shutter lag.

This also means that the EVF/LCD will display a live view image that shows the actual depth of field of the resulting image, and Focus Peaking will show an increasingly larger zone as being in focus when you stop down the lens. This can make it more difficult to nail your manual focus adjustment.

AF+MF also works with clutch-type lenses such as the XF14mm, XF16mm, or XF23mm. These lenses feature a clutch to mechanically switch between MF and AF mode. Since the focus ring of these lenses can only be turned when the clutch is in the MF position, you need the following configuration to get AF+MF to work:

- Enable AF+MF in the shooting menu.

- Select AF-S in the camera (using the focus mode switch) and MF on the lens (by pulling the clutch mechanism toward the camera).

- Use AF+MF as described above.

Here are a few tips regarding AF+MF and clutch lenses:

- Make sure that the manual focus ring of the lens has sufficient play to the left and right so you can make the necessary MF adjustments.

- The distance and DOF markings on your clutch lens have no meaning in the AF+MF configuration. Instead, use the digital distance/DOF scale that's displayed in the camera's viewfinder or on the LCD (in either PIXEL BASIS or FILM FORMAT BASIS format).

- In order to use clutch lenses in manual focus mode when AF+MF is on, both the lens *and* the camera have to be set to MF.

TIP 72	**Pre-AF:** a relic of the past

Pre-AF brings the AF-C of older Fujifilm X cameras (like the X-Pro1) to the X-T2: with Pre-AF set to ON, the camera will always focus on whatever is covered by the active AF frame, even when the shutter button is *not* half-depressed.

Pre-AF burns plenty of power because the autofocus in the lens is always working. On the other hand, using it can potentially result in a quicker AF response. If you shoot a lot of action, Pre-AF may be helpful—but don't forget to pack a few extra batteries. Normally, I set this option (AF/MF SETTING > PRE-AF) to OFF.

Using **face detection** and **eye-detection**	TIP 73

Face detection is a combined autofocus and exposure metering mode. It even affects auto white balance. You can activate it with AF/MF SETTING > FACE/EYE DETECTION SETTING and picking one of the four FACE ON options.

Here's what it does:

- The camera scans the scene and detects one or more human faces. In AF-S mode, it automatically focuses on one of the faces when the shutter button is half-pressed. When more than one face is detected, the camera tends to focus on the face that's closest to the center. That face will be highlighted with a green frame. The other detected faces will be highlighted with a white frame.

- Face detection uses a custom version of weighted multi metering that puts an emphasis on the selected face. The goal is to deliver an exposure with correct skin tones. It may also influence the camera's auto white balance.

Face detection is both a blessing and a curse. It's a blessing when it works because it focuses directly on a face and makes sure that it's correctly exposed. It's a curse when the detection goes wrong, because it doesn't just mean that the focus might miss; it may also mess up your exposure metering.

The good news is that in most cases, face detection works, even with people who only show their profiles to the camera. The bad news is that face detection may not work well on folks wearing glasses.

- If you want to take face detection exposure metering out of the equation, you can set the camera to manual exposure mode **M**. While metering will still be affected in this mode, the exposure itself will not. Alternatively, you can use the AE-L button to meter and lock the exposure and prohibit face detection from interfering with it as long as AE-L is active. You can still adjust your locked exposure with the exposure compensation dial.

- Face detection works with the full sensor area, and thus only employs CDAF. PDAF and its predictive capabilities aren't available. This means that AF-C tracking of moving objects doesn't work as well as it could. In other words, face detection isn't the best option to use when tracking an athlete or a child running toward the camera. It's better to use the camera's conventional AF-C mode with one of the central AF frames or an appropriate AF zone.

- Spot, center-weighted, and average metering aren't available when face detection is active. The camera is always using a derivate of multi metering.

- When face detection fails to detect a face in the scene, the camera will automatically fall back to the selected AF mode: Single Point, Zone, or Wide/Tracking. At the same time, exposure metering reverts back to regular multi metering.

- AF-Lock is not available when face detection is active.

- Face detection can be assigned to one of the X-T2's function (Fn) buttons. Personally, I tend to assign it to the lower selector button.

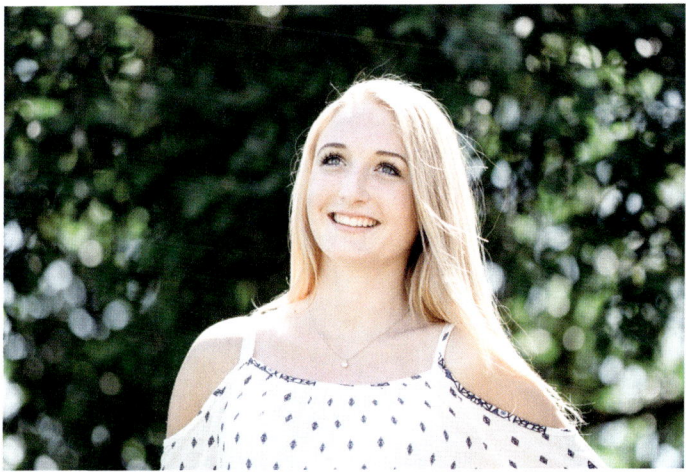

Fig. 40: **Face detection** is best for stationary scenes with one or more people looking at the camera. For people who are moving toward the camera, better use one of the central AF frames or an AF zone in concert with the X-T2's tracking autofocus (AF-C).

The X-T2 has improved face detection accuracy due to an added, optional eye-detection feature. Eye detection is only available in AF-S mode. To activate it, select either FACE ON/ LEFT EYE PRIORITY or FACE ON/RIGHT EYE PRIORITY. You can also select FACE ON/EYE AUTO to make the camera focus on the eye that's closest to the camera, or select FACE ON/ EYE OFF to deactivate eye detection during face detection.

In the viewfinder, the camera will highlight a detected eye with a small square and focus on it when you half-press the shutter button. In my experience, it doesn't hurt to leave this feature on all the time. I usually set it to EYE AUTO. However, don't forget that it's only available in AF-S mode.

Using **AF-Lock**	TIP 74

In AF-S or AF-C mode, pressing the AF-Lock button locks the current distance setting. In SET UP > BUTTON/DIAL SET- TING > AE/AF LOCK MODE, you can configure the button to function as an on/off switch (which is always my choice) or to work only as long as it is being pressed.

When AF-Lock is active, the camera won't refocus when the shutter button is half or fully depressed. Instead, it will keep the focus at the previously locked distance. This is convenient when you want to take multiple shots of a non-moving subject in quick succession. With AF-Lock, you don't have to refocus every time to take another image. AF-Lock decouples autofocus and exposure metering: as long as AF-Lock is on, half-pressing the shutter button will only meter and lock the exposure, not the focus. Of course, this only applies if SHUTTER AF (in the SET UP > BUTTON/DIAL SETTING menu) is in its default ON position.

In a similar fashion, can use the AE-Lock button to meter and lock exposure; in this case, half-pressing the shutter button will only change the focusing. You can even combine both AE-L and AF-L. In this case, half-pressing the shutter will only set the working aperture and prime the camera. There won't be any new metering for focus or exposure.

TIP 75	Using **AF-ON** (back-button focusing)

AF-ON is a new option that brings back-button focusing to the X-T2. Back-button focusing is a common practice with DSLR users. Simply put, AF-ON puts the X-T2's autofocus function on a function button. Press it, and the camera starts focusing. Stop pressing it, and the focusing stops at the current position until you press the AF-ON button again.

This means that AF-ON performs the same function as half-pressing the shutter button (assuming that SHUTTER AF ON is set in the SET UP > BUTTON/DIAL SETTING menu). In AF-S mode, pressing AF-ON will perform a single focus search and lock the target. In AF-C mode, AF-ON will continuously focus on a target as long as the button is pressed.

Since the X-T2 has no dedicated AF-ON button, it has to be assigned to a Fn button. To keep things simple and comfortable, it's best to replace the AF-L button with AF-ON. To do so, press and hold the DISP/BACK button until the Fn/ AE-L/AF-L BUTTON SETTING page appears. Scroll down to AF-L, press the right selector button and select AF-ON from the list of available functions.

You can press and hold AF-ON while you simultaneously release the shutter. In AF-S, pressing and holding AF-ON is focusing the camera and locking it as long as AF-ON is held, so simultaneously half-pressing or pressing the shutter button won't interfere with your locked focus. In AF-C, pressing and holding AF-ON means that the camera keeps tracking your target as long as AF-ON is held.

If you are a "religious" back-button-AF user (some DLSR converts are), you may find it more comfortable to entirely disable the shutter button's AF functionality by selecting SET UP > BUTTON/DIAL SETTING > SHUTTER AF > OFF, meaning AF-ON will be the only available method to auto-focus in AF-S or AF-C mode.

In manual focus (MF) mode, AF-ON turns into Instant AF (One-Touch-AF), just like the normal AF-L button.

Focusing in poor light	TIP 76

Low light can quickly lead to poor contrast, making it difficult for the camera to find and lock the correct autofocus distance. However, the amount of light that reaches the sensor depends not only on the brightness of a scene, but also on the brightness of the lens. The XF56mmF1.2 is 3.5 stops or EVs (exposure values) brighter than the XF18–55mmF2.8–4 kit zoom in its 55mm position. In other words, with the XF56mmF1.2 lens, the world looks 3.5 stops brighter to the camera's autofocus system. You can guess which lens will perform better when the light gets difficult.

Don't be confused by appearances—it's true that the live view image in the viewfinder will look equally bright with both lenses, but that's only because the camera is electronically amplifying the live view display. Don't forget that autofocus needs *real* light and contrast. When the light is bad, it's vital to target surfaces with contrast and, if possible, use a larger AF frame size.

One way of tackling a bad lighting situation is by using fast lenses, like the XF56mmF1.2, XF35mmF1.4, or XF23mmF1.4. You can also generate light—the camera's AF assist lamp can illuminate a subject to help the autofocus find better contrast. Be aware that the AF assist lamp can be easily blocked by an attached lens hood. Watch for it, and remove the lens hood if necessary. Since the AF assist lamp tends to concentrate on the center of the image, it works best in concert with one of the more central AF frames. In order to use the AF assist lamp, make sure to set AF/MF SETTING > AF ILLUMINATOR > ON.

An alternative to using the AF assist lamp is using a flashlight to temporarily illuminate a subject. If you are indoors, you can try turning on the lights in the room for a moment and use AF-Lock to lock the focus. Just make sure to meter the exposure *after* the lights are off again.

Important: If you intend to stop down the aperture of your lens in poor lighting, make sure to use either AF-S or manual focus (Instant AF) as your focus mode. Do not use AF-C, because this mode will focus with your stopped-down working aperture, which will make things difficult for your camera since less light will reach the sensor.

TIP 77	Macro: focusing at close distances

The biggest challenge with shooting macro is the lack of depth of field. The slightest movement may cause the shot to be out of focus. That's why macro photography is usually performed using a tripod and manual focus, often with One-Touch-AF, focus check (magnifier tool), and focus peaking. It's vital not to recompose after the focus has been set. To get a visual impression of the current DOF, you can half-press the shutter or assign PREVIEW DEPTH OF FIELD to one of the Fn buttons.

Macro shots usually require you to stop down the lens in order to increase the DOF. Since this can result in slower shutter speeds, it's important to make sure that the subject isn't moving too fast or out of the focus plane. Shooting a close-up of a flower in the wind may not yield excellent results.

If you don't want to use manual focus in macro mode, you can also focus automatically. Here's how:

- Set the focus selector switch to AF-S.

- Set Single Point AF and select the smallest AF frame size available.

- Reposition the small AF frame to exactly cover the part of the image that you want to be in focus. Quickly take the shot after you half-press the shutter—don't recompose. Don't forget that your X-T2 offers you the opportunity to use 325 instead of 91 AF frames in Single Point AF mode. This may be the time to use this option.

- You can check your focus before taking a shot by pressing the rear command dial. After doing so, you can change the magnification factor by turning the command dial.

- Try not to shoot hand-held; it's better to use a tripod.

- Stop down the lens and visually check the depth of field by half-pressing the shutter button or using the DOF preview function (remember that function can be assigned to any Fn button).

- Make sure there is sufficient light, and try to shoot subjects that don't move in and out of the focus plane.

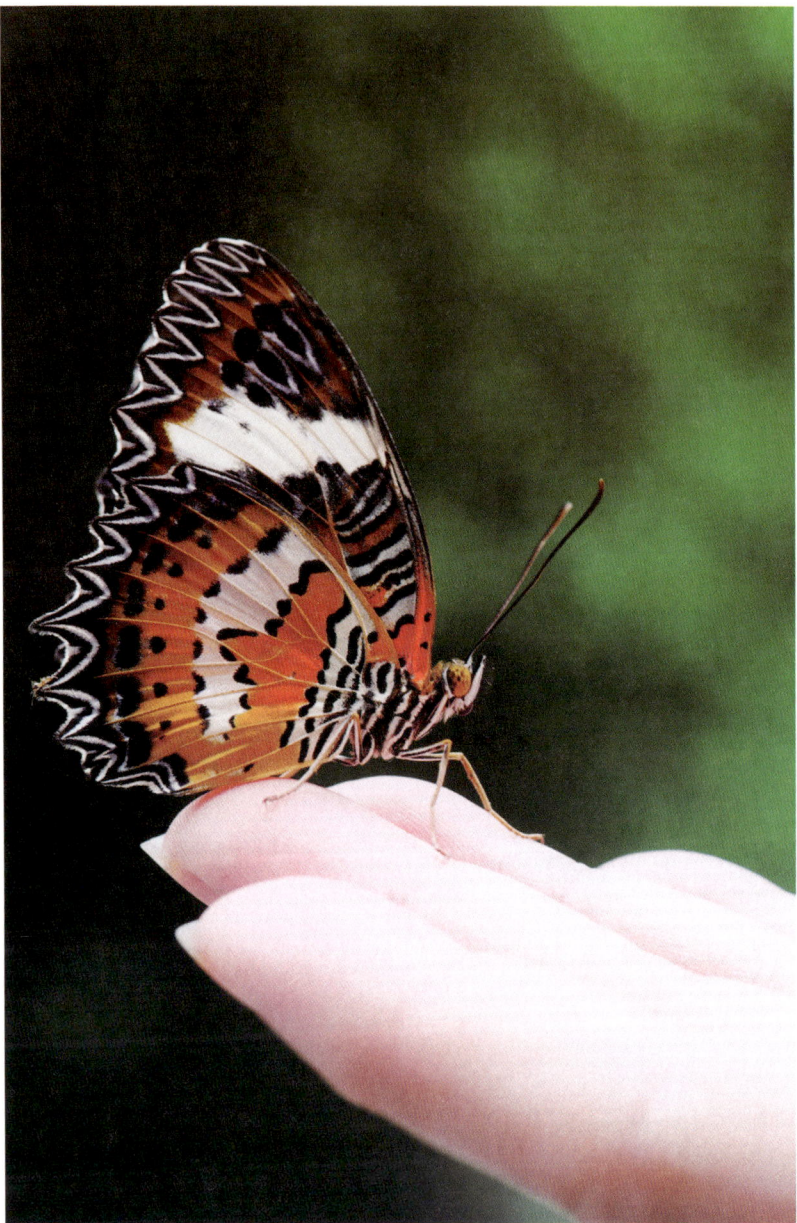

Fig. 41: **Macro shots** can be quite challenging due to their lack of DOF. That's why a tripod is highly recommended. With a little bit of luck, hand-held shots are possible, as well. This handheld snapshot was taken in 2012 with the classic X-Pro1 and an XF60mmF2.4 R.

You can add macro capability to many of your existing XF and XC lenses by using Fujifilm's electronic macro extension tubes: MCEX-11 or MCEX-16. This PDF file [49] will provide a chart that shows how these extension tubes enhance the magnification factor of each lens. Please note that the camera's electronic DOF/distance scale doesn't reflect the use of macro extension tubes.

Focusing on moving subjects (1): the "autofocus trick"	TIP 78

Rule of thumb: Use AF-S (Single) for stationary subjects; use AF-C (Continuous) for subjects that move toward or away from the camera. But, as usual, there's no rule without an exception: meet the so-called "autofocus trick" or "shutter mash" technique:

■ Set the focus selector switch to AF-S and the camera to single shot (S) using the DRIVE dial. Make sure that Boost mode is on. You might also want to use PRE-AF in this particular case. Last but not least, make sure to use the mechanical shutter.

■ Use Single Point AF or Zone AF. Select an AF frame or zone position and size that cover the part of the moving subject you want to be in focus. If possible, use the inner AF frames, which, as you know, are PDAF-enabled. However, it's definitely possible to also use the outer frames that only operate with CDAF. If your composition requires them, go for it!

■ Set a suitable exposure and make sure that the shutter speed is fast enough to avoid unwanted motion blur. Most action shots require shutter speeds of at least 1/1000s.

■ Follow the moving subject in the viewfinder, making sure that the selected AF frame or AF zone always covers the part that needs to be in focus. Do *not* half-press the shutter button!

■ *Fully* depress the shutter button in one swift motion when you want to take the shot. The camera will need some time to focus, so make sure the AF frame stays positioned over the moving subject while the camera is focusing. As soon as the camera is able to lock focus, it will automatically take the shot. This time between fully depressing the shutter and the camera taking the shot can take a good fraction of a second.

The AF trick or shutter mash is based on the camera's autofocus priority logic. When you release the shutter, the camera *first* attempts to lock the focus, *then* take the shot. Since the delay between having locked the focus and releasing the shutter is very short, the moving subject ends up being in focus most of the time. This means that the AF trick works best with aperture settings that offer sufficient depth of field, and with subjects that don't move too fast toward the camera.

A negative aspect of this method is the delay between fully depressing the shutter button and the camera taking the shot. This makes it challenging to hit decisive moments, and requires some amount of foresight from the photographer.

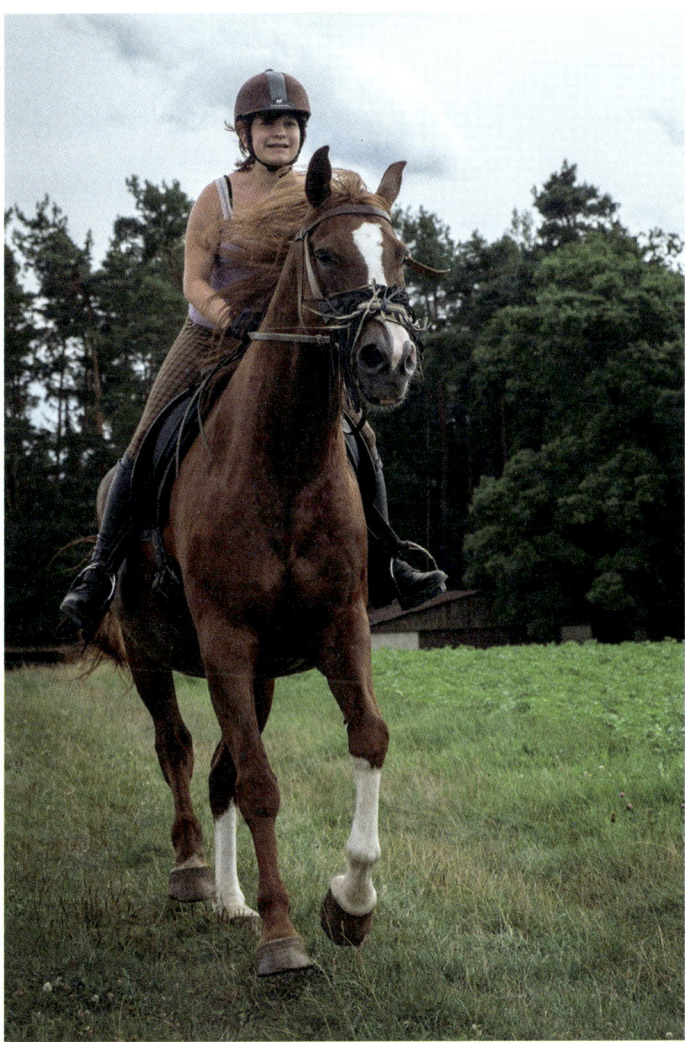

Fig. 42: A running horse captured using the **autofocus trick** or shutter mash technique. With older X-mount models like the X-Pro1, X-E1, X-M1, X-A1, or X-A2, this method is the only way to capture subjects (using the camera's autofocus) that are moving toward the camera. This sample image was taken with an X-E1.

| TIP 79 | Focusing on moving subjects (2): **the focus trap** |

Setting up a focus trap is about pre-focusing on a location that a moving object will eventually pass through. This method can be useful with sports and other action that runs along a pre-determined course (track, street, trail, etc.).

This is how it works:

- Set the camera to manual focus (MF) using the focus selector switch. Make sure to use the mechanical shutter.

- Pre-focus on the location where you want to capture the moving subject. Select an aperture with sufficient depth of field (DOF) to make sure that all relevant parts of the object will be in focus.

- Half-press the shutter button when the moving object is approaching the location you have in focus. The camera will lock the exposure and set the working aperture.

- Fully depress the shutter as soon as the object is about to cross the in-focus location.

There's only a very small shutter lag between half-pressing and fully depressing the shutter button. Depending on how fast the object is moving, it may be necessary to fully depress the shutter button a split second early.

Alternatively, you can set the camera to burst mode (set the DRIVE dial to CH). With this setting, the X-T2 takes 8 or 11 frames per second (fps), so there's a good chance that one or two of them will capture your fast-moving subject as it crosses your focus trap.

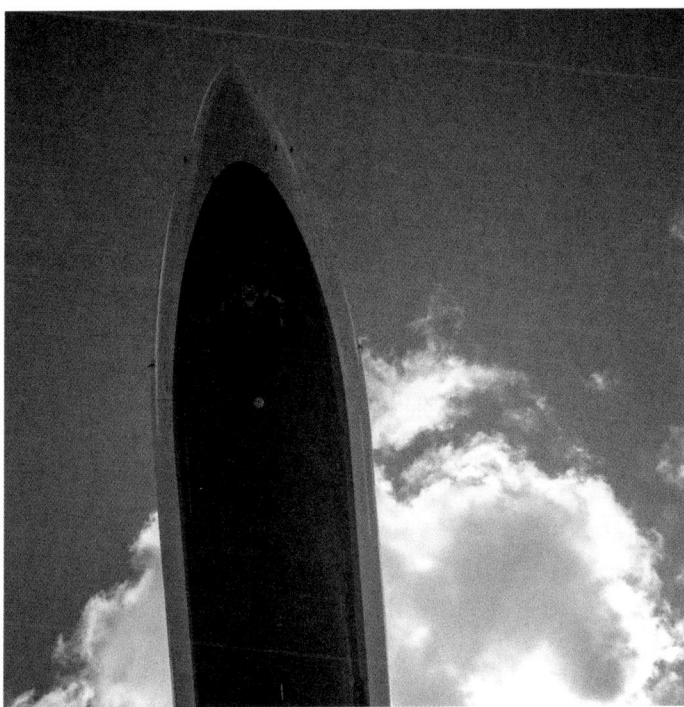

Fig. 43: **Focus trap:** To capture this landing Airbus A330 as it was flying over me at a distance of only a few meters, timing was essential. Instead of using autofocus, I pre-focused my 18mm lens with sufficient depth of field and waited for the right moment with my camera primed and the shutter half-pressed.

You can also trap your moving subjects in a set-up focus zone. Stop down your lens enough to create a sufficiently large DOF zone, and then wait until a subject enters the zone. This method is often used by street photographers with wide-angle lenses (typically 18–23mm) who can't afford to miss the decisive moment.

A variant of this method is panning [12] the camera with a slow shutter speed and a small aperture (plenty of DOF). The slow shutter speed makes sure that the background is blurred while the subject remains in focus.

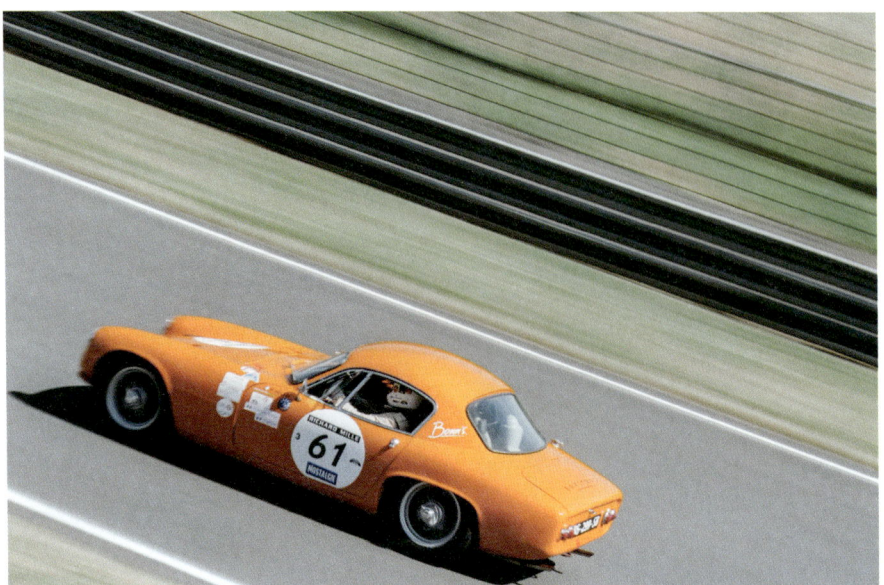

Fig. 44: **Panning** the camera in-synch with a racecar at 1/60s: the slow shutter speed resulted in f/18 and more than sufficient DOF using a focal length of 50mm.

TIP 80	Focusing on moving subjects (3): **Autofocus tracking using Single Point AF, Zone AF, or Wide/Tracking AF**

The predictive PDAF of your X-T2 uses the 49 or 169 (depending on your NUMBER OF FOCUS POINTS setting) central AF points. Predictive PDAF allows you to track moving subjects with your camera in three-dimensional space. Since the camera is able to calculate the movement of the object, it can automatically pre-focus on its future position and compensate for any inherent shutter lag.

The X-T2 also improves the predictive capabilities of the CDAF. This means that subject tracking is also available with AF frames that surround the central PDAF points, as long as the burst rate in continuous shooting mode doesn't exceed 5 frames per second. It's important to note that the hit rate of such predictions is never near 100%, but it's accurate enough to deliver good results in concert with the camera's burst mode settings.

Let's start with the **Single Point AF** and **Zone AF** modes:

■ Set the focus mode selector switch to AF-C and make sure that Boost mode is on. Also make sure that the shutter type is set to the mechanical shutter (MS) in the shooting menu.

■ Set the camera to burst mode (set the DRIVE dial to CL or CH). I recommend using the slower CL mode, since it displays a real-time live view image between shots and supports all AF frames.

■ If you are using Single Point AF, select one of the central PDAF-enabled autofocus frames. If you use one of the outer AF frames, the camera will only use CDAF. In concert with one of the outer AF frames, you can only use the slower of the two burst modes (CL). You should still get pretty good results, though.

■ If you are using Zone AF, select a zone that doesn't extend beyond the central 7×7 AF point matrix. If you use a zone that includes AF points beyond this PDAF-enabled area, the camera can only use CDAF, and only the slower of the two burst modes (CL) is available.

■ Position the selected AF frame or AF zone to directly cover the subject or part of the subject that you want in focus. Half-press the shutter button, and the camera will start tracking the subject covered by the AF frame or AF zone.

■ Keep the shutter button half-depressed as you follow the moving subject with the selected AF frame or AF zone.

■ Fully depress the shutter when you want to start taking a series of exposures. The actual burst speed (frame rate) depends on how well the camera is able to track the subject. As the camera is taking pictures, keep the selected AF frame or AF Zone over the part of your image that is supposed to be in focus. This may be challenging at first, so practicing is important.

In the above configuration with burst mode and AF-C, the X-T2 is not adjusting the exposure between shots when SHUTTER AE is set to ON. White balance and dynamic range settings are also determined with the first shot and remain constant throughout the series.

If you want the camera to adjust exposure between shots in burst mode, select SET UP > BUTTON/DIAL SETTING > SHUTTER AE > OFF.

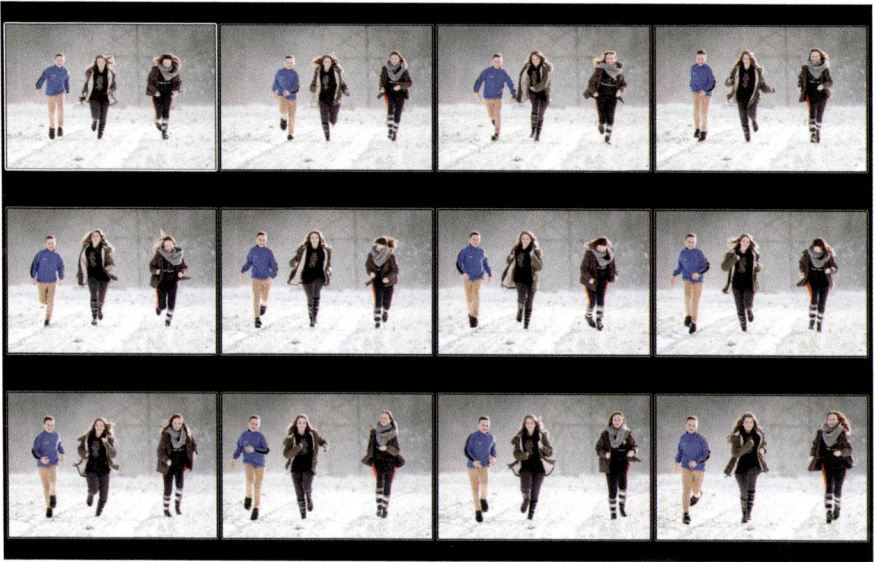

Fig. 45: **AF tracking** with AF-C and burst mode: The predictive autofocus was tracking one of the kids with the selected AF zone while they were running toward the camera. To make this kind of shot work, it's vital to follow the subject with the active AF frame or AF zone, making sure it's always covering the part of the subject that is supposed to be in focus.

In principle, AF-C tracking also works in single shot mode (DRIVE dial set to S, not to be confused with the AF mode selector). In this case, the camera takes a single frame when the shutter button is fully depressed, then ends the tracking.

By the way, it is perfectly normal for the hybrid AF to continuously hunt in the viewfinder during focus tracking (in AF-C mode). Don't be irritated by the live view image changing between in focus and not in focus. It's all about the results.

As an alternative to Single Point and Zone AF, you can also use **Wide/Tracking AF** in concert with AF-C to track a moving subject. This mode enables real 3D tracking, meaning the camera isn't merely tracking a subject's changing distance to the camera (z-axis), but also its left/right (x-axis) und up/down (y-axis) movement within the image frame.

Here's how it works:

■ Set the focus mode selector switch to AF-C and make sure that Boost mode is on. Also make sure that the shutter type is set to the mechanical shutter (MS) in the shooting menu.

■ Set the camera to **Wide/Tracking AF** and select the slower of the two burst modes (set the DRIVE dial menu to CL). That way, 3D tracking will be available for the *entire* image frame, but it will only track objects using CDAF. If you set the DRIVE dial to CH, tracking will use PDAF, but will be limited to the smaller PDAF-enabled central area.

■ Select one of the up to 91 available tracking AF points. The point you select will serve as a starting point for your tracking action, so position it in a way that suits your composition.

■ To identify your target, make sure that the selected AF point covers the object you want to track and half-press the shutter button. As long as you keep the shutter button half-pressed, the camera will use pattern recognition to automatically follow the object as it moves around the frame (or as you move the camera around) with a cloud of small green AF frames.

■ Fully depress the shutter button and keep it pressed to take pictures at the selected burst rate.

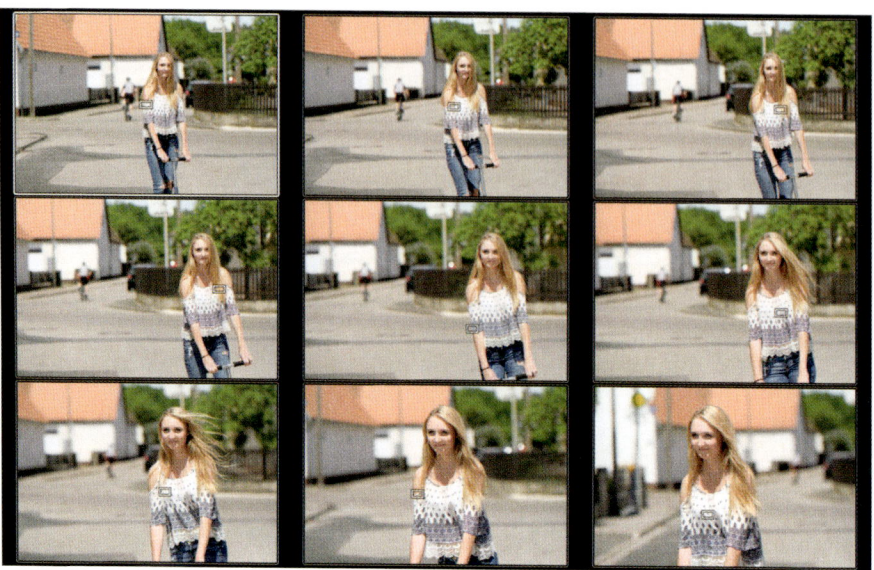

Fig. 46: AF-C in concert with **WIDE/TRACKING** and burst mode can track a subject in 3-dimensional space. To accomplish this, the X-T2 is using pattern recognition to follow the designated subject as it moves.

TIP 81	Using **AF-C Custom settings**

Your X-T2 features three parameters that allow you to customize the AF-C for a specific task or application:

■ **Tracking Sensitivity** (TS) specifies whether the camera should switch its focus to a different subject or retain its focus to wait for the subject to reappear. This control is useful when the subject you are tracking disappears behind an obstacle or goes out of the frame, or when a second object at a substantially different distance from the subject comes into the frame. Selecting 0 makes the camera switch its focus immediately, while choosing 1–4 progressively lengthens the time it will retain focus. Technically speaking, tracking sensitivity 0 will not predict an autofocus target's position when it's temporarily lost or obscured by something else. Tracking sensitivity settings of 1, 2, 3, and 4 will predict a lost or obscured target's position for another 0.4 seconds, 0.7 seconds, 1.0 second, and 1.3 seconds, respectively, before the AF-C looks for a new tracking target.

■ **Speed Tracking Sensitivity** (STS) controls the camera's tracking characteristics based on changes to the subject's speed. Selecting 0 (constant speed), the camera expects a steady movement when it predicts the subject's distance. Select 1 or 2, and the camera takes speed changes more and more into account when it's predicting subject movement, making it suitable for accelerating or decelerating targets like rapidly accelerating and decelerating race cars.

■ **Zone Area Switching** (ZAS) is available only in the Zone AF mode and specifies which part of the selected focusing zone should be given focusing priority. Select CENTER to maintain focus in the center of the zone. Set FRONT to switch the focus to the closest subject in the zone, which is great for capturing new targets that suddenly move into a zone. AUTO tracks the subject you first focused on.

You can set these parameters individually, or you can choose from several presets to cover typical AF-C shooting scenarios. Select AF/MF SETTING > AF-C CUSTOM SETTINGS, then pick one of six available sets:

■ SET 1: MULTI PURPOSE is the default setting and is our general AF-C setting. It also corresponds to the AF-C setting on previous models like the X-Pro2, and it's a great choice for situations where you don't have a clear understanding of how different custom settings could improve the AF-C performance. Its parameter settings are TS 2, STS 0, and ZAS AUTO.

■ SET 2: IGNORE OBSTACLES & CONTINUE TO TRACK SUBJECT keeps the focus on a subject even when it's temporarily going out of the frame or is obscured by obstacles.

This can be useful for following a specific target with the camera and ensuring that the target isn't lost when it's temporarily obscured by people, trees and other obstacles that pass through the line of sight. Its parameter settings are TS 3, STS 0, and ZAS CENTER.

■ SET 3: FOR ACCELERATING/DECELERATING SUBJECT is your typical racetrack mode. It takes changing relative speeds of subjects moving towards the camera into account. Whenever you have targets than rapidly accelerate or decelerate, this mode can be useful, especially in concert with XF lenses featuring high-speed linear autofocus motors. Its parameter settings are TS 2, STS 2, and ZAS AUTO.

■ SET 4: FOR SUDDENLY APPEARING SUBJECT allows the camera to instantly focus on a subject that comes into the focusing area, with priority given to objects closest to the camera. It is ideal for subjects that suddenly appear in the focusing frame. Its parameter settings are TS 0, STS 1, and ZAS FRONT.

■ SET 5: FOR ERRATICALY MOVING & ACCEL./DECEL. SUBJECT is suitable for subjects that are moving at varying speeds in different directions, coming in and out of the focusing area. It is perfect for shooting field sports like soccer. Its parameter settings are TS 3, STS 2, and ZAS AUTO.

■ SET 6: CUSTOM stores your individual settings for the three AF-C subject tracking parameters TRACKING SENSITIVITY (TS), SPEED TRACKING SENSITIVITY (STS), and ZONE AREA SWITCHING (ZAS). Use this preset to manually create optimized settings for the specific movement characteristics of your subject.

Focus priority vs. release priority	TIP 82

The autofocus in your X-T2 will *always* try to focus on a subject before the camera takes the shot. In this context, release priority vs. focus priority only refers to how the camera is behaving when the AF *fails* to lock on a target:

- Set AF/MF SETTING > RELEASE/FOCUS PRIORITY > AF-S PRIORITY SELECTION > FOCUS to stop the camera from taking a picture when the autofocus (AF-S) can't lock onto a target (red AF warning).

- Set AF/MF SETTING > RELEASE/FOCUS PRIORITY > AF-C PRIORITY SELECTION > FOCUS to make sure that the X-T2 only takes pictures in AF-C mode (particularly in concert with burst mode) when the autofocus is able to lock onto something.

Basically, selecting focus priority for AF-S and AF-C reduces the number of out-of-focus pictures on your memory card.

By default, the camera is set to release priority, following the motto, "better a misfocused shot than no image at all." Since I am no friend of misfocused shots, my X-T2 is set to focus priority for both AF-S and AF-C.

Please note that when AF+MF is active in AF-S mode, the camera will always use AF-S Release Priority.

2.5 WHITE BALANCE AND JPEG PARAMETERS

A great feature of all X-series cameras is their ability to set white balance [50] and JPEG parameters before you take a shot and after, using the built-in RAW converter. This gives you full control over the JPEGs that are generated in the camera.

It's not necessary to anticipate and set the perfect settings for each shot in advance because you can generate different JPEG versions of a shot with the internal RAW converter. For example, you could create a version with bold Velvia colors, or a black-and-white version with strong contrast and minimal noise reduction. As long as you have access to the RAW file, you can change all JPEG parameters after the fact and generate as many different-looking JPEGs as you want.

Using the built-in RAW converter in the playback menu is quite easy because it offers the same functions that are available in shooting mode (in the IMAGE QUALITY SET-TING menu).

IMAGE QUALITY SETTING menu	RAW CONVERSION menu
(Exposure Comp. Dial)	PUSH/PULL PROCESSING
DYNAMIC RANGE	DYNAMIC RANGE
FILM SIMULATION	FILM SIMULATION
WHITE BALANCE	WHITE BALANCE
(incl. WB SHIFT)	WB SHIFT
COLOR	COLOR
SHARPNESS	SHARPNESS
HIGHLIGHT TONE	HIGHLIGHT TONE
SHADOW TONE	SHADOW TONE
NOISE REDUCTION	NOISE REDUCTION
GRAIN EFFECT	GRAIN EFFECT
LENS MODULATION OPTIMIZER	LENS MODULATION OPTIMIZER
COLOR SPACE	COLOR SPACE

The only relevant differences affect the first two items in this list:

- **Exposure corrections** made *before* you take a picture can affect aperture, shutter speed, and ISO. **Push/pull processing** *after* you have taken a picture only affects the ISO amplification. Changing the ISO via push/pull processing also doesn't change the ISO value in the EXIF data [21] of the JPEGs. Push/Pull processing in the internal RAW converter is the same as moving the exposure slider in external RAW conversion software, such as Lightroom, Silkypix, or Capture One.

■ *Before* you take an image, you can select four different **dynamic range** options: AUTO, DR100%, DR200%, or DR400%. DR200% exposes the RAW file one stop lower than normal; DR400% exposes it two stops lower. DR-Auto automatically selects either DR100% or DR200%. *After* you have taken an image, you can still select different DR settings in the internal RAW converter. However, you can only *reduce* the DR, not increase it. If you are working on a RAW file that was recorded with DR400%, you can reprocess it to create JPEGs with DR400%, DR200%, or DR100%. A DR200% RAW file can be reprocessed with DR200% or DR100%, but not DR400%. A DR100% RAW file can only be reprocessed with DR100%.

The correct **white balance** ensures that white or gray areas of an image appear white or gray (without color tints) regardless of the light conditions. At the same time, the results are usually not supposed to look clinically neutral. The X-T2 masters this task quite well, so you can rely on the Auto white balance setting to get it right most of the time.

However, "most of the time" is not "all the time." There are instances when the white balance is off, or when you *want* it to be off. For example, you may want to emphasize a sunset with a warmer white balance. In such cases, it makes perfect sense to manually set the white balance in advance.

The X-T2 offers a variety of options to manually set the white balance:

■ Seven white balance presets for typical situations, such as sunny weather (Fine), cloudy skies (Shade), or tungsten light (Incandescent)

■ A Kelvin option to manually set the color temperature

■ Custom white balance that actually meters a white or neutral surface (like a white wall) under the current light conditions. This way, the camera can adjust the white balance to make the surface appear neutral.

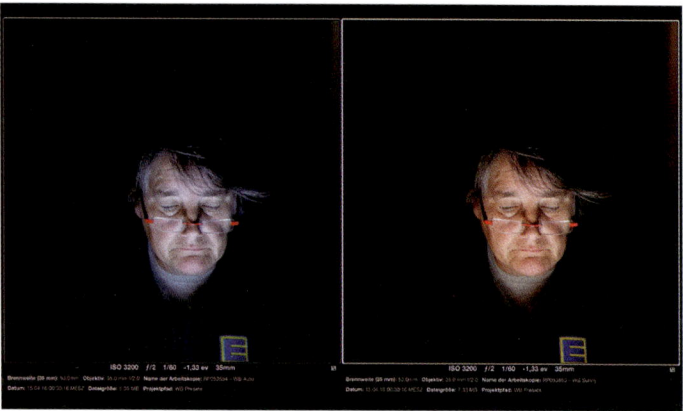

Fig. 47: Two versions of the same shot, taken with different **white balance settings.** Illuminated by an iPad screen, the left image shows the somewhat cool Auto setting; the right image shows the warmer Sunny preset.

TIP 83	Custom white balance: a little effort can go a long way

This useful function is only available *before* you take a shot, because you are metering the white balance of the actual scene. Custom white balance allows you to calibrate the camera's white balance toward a specific object that you want to appear neutral in the final image.

Here we go:

■ Select IMAGE QUALITY SETTING > WHITE BALANCE > CUSTOM(1–3) and press the RIGHT SELECTOR KEY (right arrow).

■ Point the camera toward a surface that you want to use as a neutral reference, for example a white wall or a gray card [51]. Make sure that the surface is large enough to be fully covered by the white balance metering frame in the viewfinder. Come closer to your subject or zoom in if you need to.

■ Fully press the shutter button to meter and set the new custom white balance. The live view will change accordingly and simulate the adjusted color temperature. If you are happy with the result, confirm it by pressing the OK button.

You can use the same procedure with a firing flash unit. In this case, the custom white balance will meter the mix of flash-light and surrounding light that hits your neutral reference surface.

Don't worry! You are under no obligation to use the custom white balance later during RAW conversion. It's simply one of many options, and you can always adjust it later as you please. For example, you can use the built-in RAW converter with a manual KELVIN setting or one of seven white balance presets (FINE, SHADE, FLUORESCENT LIGHT 1–3, INCANDESCENT, and UNDERWATER). You can even use AUTO white balance anytime later because the camera will always save its automatic white balance metering for later use in the internal RAW converter.

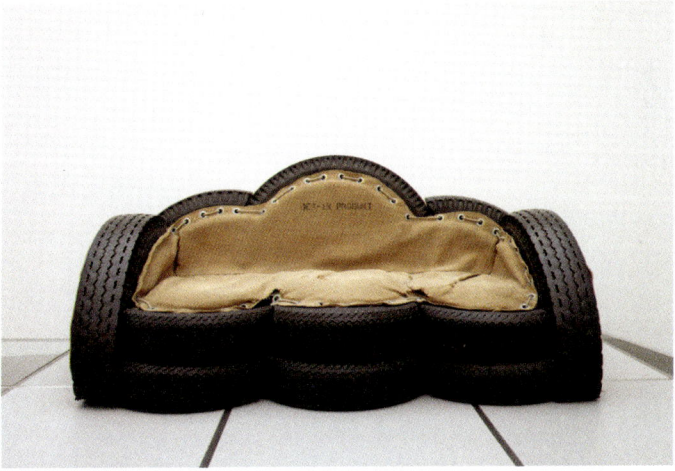

Fig. 48: A **custom white balance** setting was used to take this shot. The wall behind the sofa served as a neutral reference.

TIP 84 | Infrared photography

Since the X-T2 features a weak IR-blocking filter in front of its sensor, it's quite suitable for infrared photography. You'll need an infrared filter in front of your lens, typically of the R72 kind, which is available from Hoya and other filter vendors. This filter blocks all light wavelengths except infrared, making sure only infrared light reaches the sensor.

To minimize the resulting red tint in the live view (and JPEGs), set the color temperature to the minimum of 2500 Kelvin. You can also select one of the eight different black-and-white film simulation modes to completely eliminate colors in the viewfinder (and JPEGs).

Since the R72 filter blocks a large amount of light, it's useful to shoot with a tripod.

Fig. 49: (Opposite page) This **infrared image** by X-Photographer Mehrdad Abedi was processed in Adobe Lightroom and shot with a R72 filter (Credit: www.qimago.de).

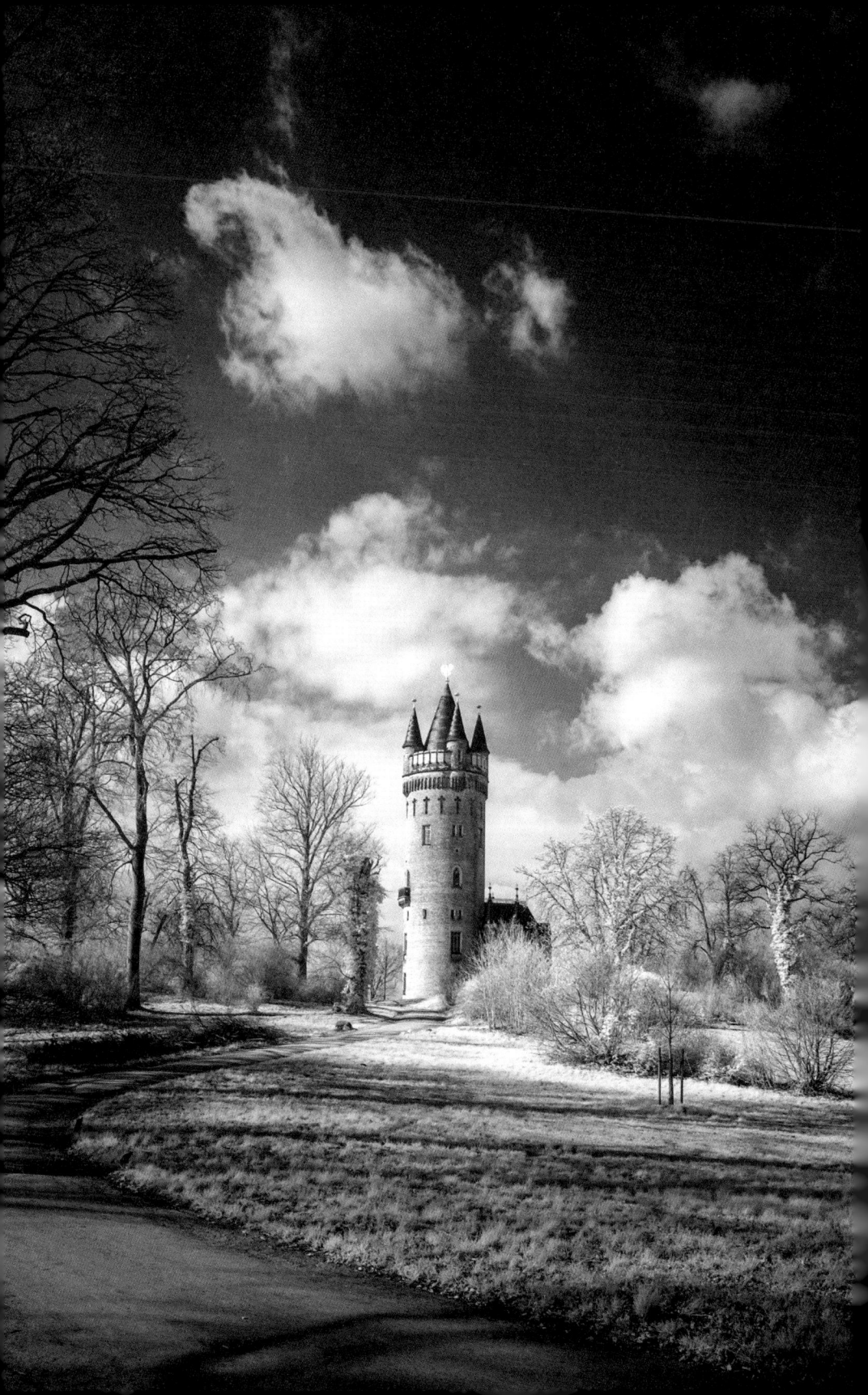

TIP 85 Changing color tints with **WB SHIFT**

WB SHIFT offers the opportunity to correct (or introduce) color tint in any shot. You can adjust the color tint as an add-on to every white balance setting—either before you take a shot or in the built-in RAW converter.

You can set a *different* white balance shift for each of the X-T2's white balance options (Auto, Kelvin, the seven presets, and the three Custom white balance settings). You can do this by changing the tint between green and red on the X-axis and between yellow and blue on the Y-axis of the display that automatically appears when you select one of the twelve white balance options.

I recommend a neutral setting here to avoid confusion. As mentioned before, there's a different white balance shift setting for each of the white balance options, meaning the camera can store twelve different white balance shift settings at once. This makes it easy to forget a previously set correction, which is why I recommend introducing white balance shift during RAW conversion. Here's where you can actually see, for example, that the skin tones in a portrait may require an adjustment.

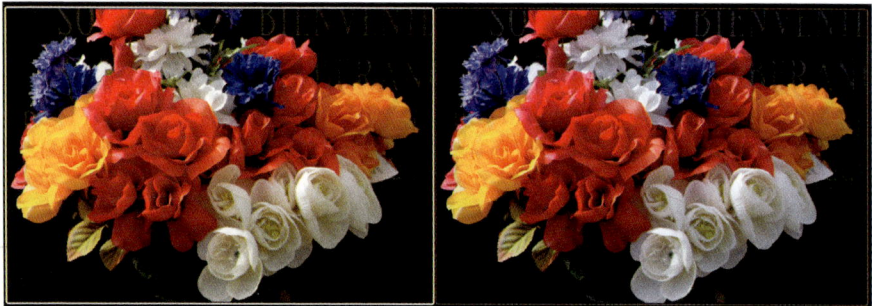

Fig. 50: **WB SHIFT in action:** The example on the left shows the image with AUTO white balance and factory JPEG settings. On the right you can see the same image, again with AUTO white balance and factory settings, but with a manual WB SHIFT of Blue +6 and RED −3 to make it look colder than the original.

Film simulations: it's all about the look.	TIP 86

The importance of film simulations for the overall look of a JPEG is often underestimated. Film simulations influence color grading, color saturation, dynamic range, and contrast in the resulting JPEGs. Picking a film simulation is always my first step when I'm adjusting JPEG parameters. As with all JPEG parameters, film simulations have no effect on the actual RAW file (the digital negative). Instead, they only affect the JPEGs that are generated in the camera (the digital prints). The X-T2 offers six different color film simulations, eight black-and-white modes, and one sepia option:

- PROVIA is the standard, all-purpose setting of your X-T2. The name reminds us of Fuji's popular Provia slide film.

- ASTIA is another color slide film derivate with softer highlights and pleasing skin tones. It's often used for portraits, but can also work with landscape shots that feature a lot of vegetation. A special treat of this film simulation is its bluish shadows.

- VELVIA is a very contrast-heavy, color-saturated derivate of the legendary Fuji Velvia slide film. It's mostly used for landscape and nature shots and is definitely not the best choice for portrait work.

- CLASSIC CHROME is Fuji's latest color film simulation. It has already become quite popular. That's understandable, since it reminds us of the golden era of *LIFE* magazine color photography. The distinctive look of Classic Chrome is equally suitable for landscapes and portraits.

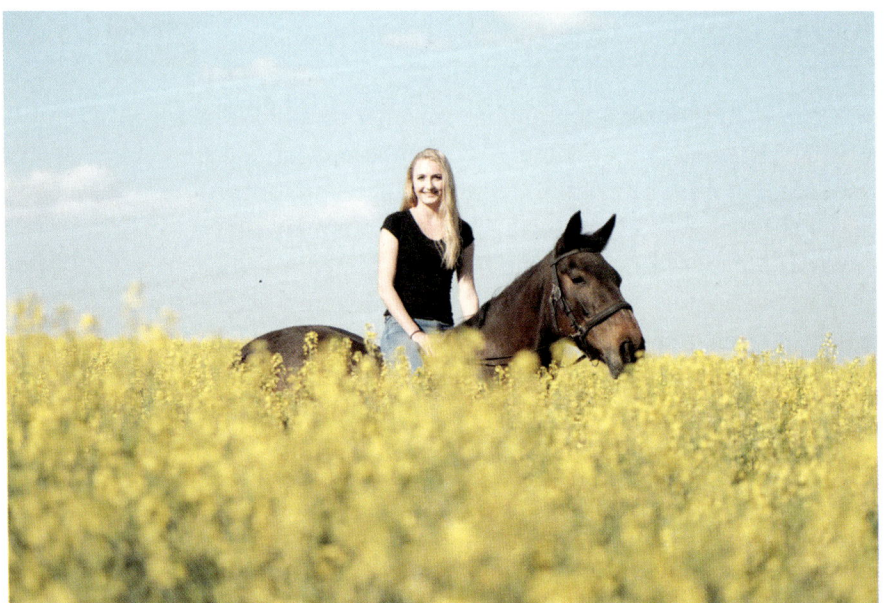

Fig. 51: The distinctive look of **CLASSIC CHROME** has earned it much popularity in a very short time.

- PRO NEG. HI is derived from a negative film that was specifically made for portraits. It delivers accurate and pleasing skin tones with nice contrast, adding some punch to the image.

- PRO NEG. STD is the most neutral film simulation of the X-T2. Featuring flat contrast, subdued colors, and high dynamic range, it can look dull at first, but the JPEGs are usable for further post-processing. Fuji recommends this film simulation for studio portraits in a flash setup.

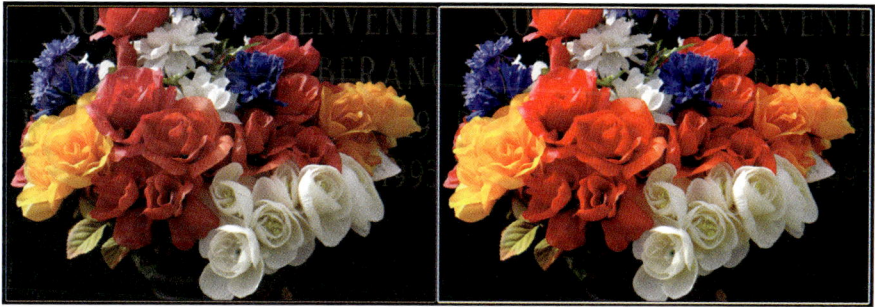

Fig. 52: **Antagonists:** PRO NEG. STD and VELVIA illustrate the spectrum of Fuji's different film simulation modes. On the left you can see the PRO NEG. STD version of a shot, and on the right its VELVIA cousin.

- MONOCHROME is Fuji's standard black-and-white conversion. Black-and-white photography depends on different gray levels being assigned to different colors. In order to increase the contrast, many photographers combine MONOCHROME with increased SHADOW TONE and HIGHLIGHT TONE settings. Additionally, noise reduction is decreased to reveal more detail and display more noise, which gives the appearance of film grain.

- MONOCHROME+Ye FILTER adds a digital yellow filter to the black-and-white conversion. This typically results in a slight increase of contrast because yellow parts of the color images will be represented by brighter gray tones.

- MONOCHROME+R FILTER adds a red filter to the black-and-white conversion. This means that skin tones will become brighter, which will camouflage reddish skin impurities. Conversely, blue skies will be darkened, adding contrast between clouds and the sky.

- MONOCHROME+G FILTER adds a green filter to the black-and-white conversion. This filter will add texture to skin tones and can potentially emphasize impurities.

- SEPIA results in a sepia-toned monochrome JPEG for an antique touch.

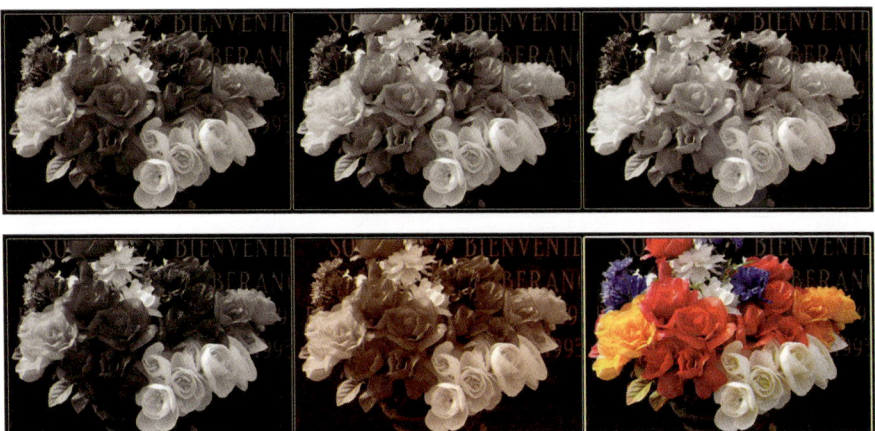

Fig. 53: **Comparing B&W options:** From left to right, first row: un-filtered B&W, yellow filter, and red filter. Second row: green filter, sepia, and the original shot in color.

- ACROS is Fuji's latest black-and-white film simulation and a great alternative to the regular MONOCHROME settings. ACROS is also available in four versions (no filter, or with either a yellow, red, or green filter). It reminds us of Fujifilm's analog film of the same name and offers a particularly cinematic look. This is partly because ACROS includes an ISO-dependent analog film grain simulation that transforms regular noise into analog-looking film grain. This special "noise shaping" is only available in the camera's built-in processor and can't be replicated with external RAW converters.

The best way to learn about film simulations is to use and compare the different options. The easiest way to do so is with the camera's internal RAW converter. Take the RAW file of a shot and process it with all available film simulations, then import the JPEGs into your computer and compare them on your monitor.

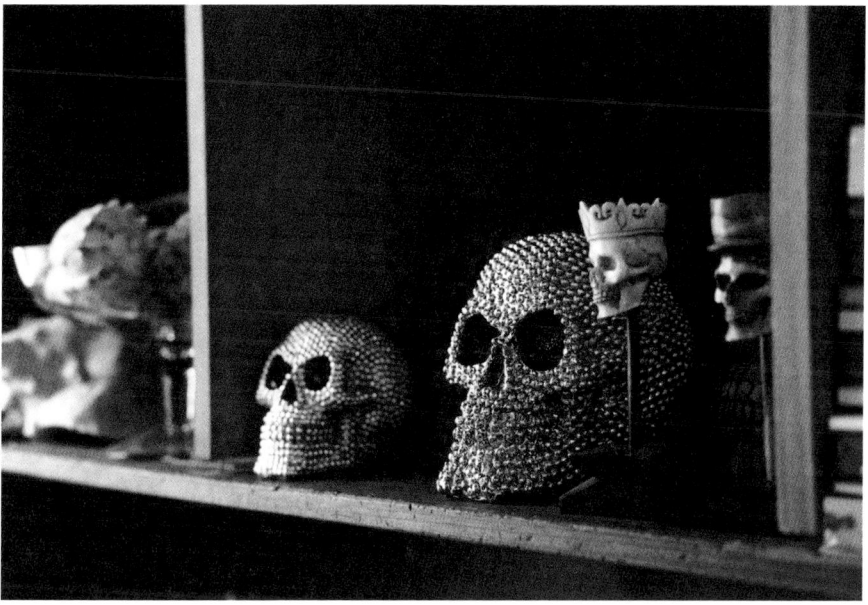

Fig. 54: Even at ISO 25600, the noise shaping of the **ACROS film simulation** delivers a natural-looking result with high resolution and fine details.

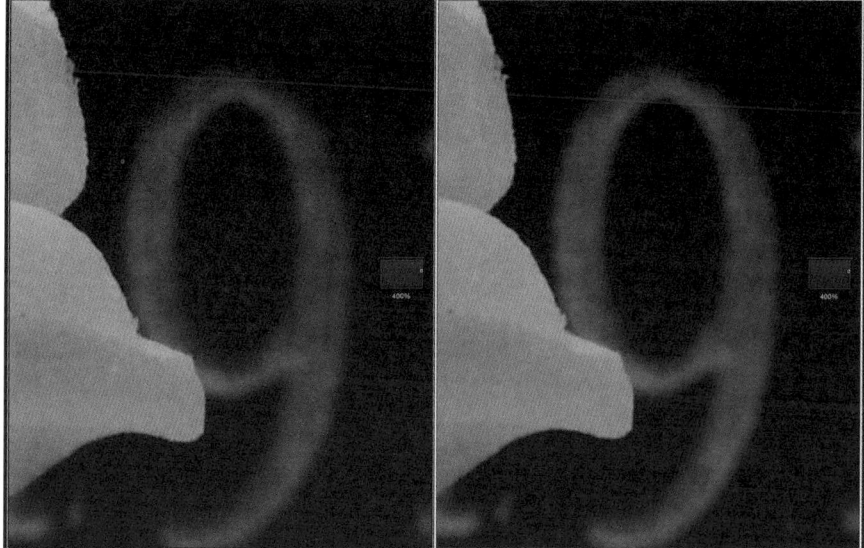

Fig. 55: ACROS offers ISO-dependent **analog film grain simulation** based on innovative noise shaping. Even at base-ISO 200, there's already a subtle difference between ACROS (left image) and the regular MONOCHROME film simulation (right image).

TIP 87	Using the **GRAIN EFFECT**

Fujifilm is all about great film simulations with an organic look, so adding "analog film grain" to a digital image can be useful to achieve a more natural look with enhanced micro contrast.

The X-T2's JPEG engine offers two GRAIN EFFECT options: WEAK and STRONG. Unlike ACROS, these options don't transform noise into analog-looking film grain; they simply add a layer of randomized, simulated film grain to the image. It's an ISO-independent add-on effect that can be used with all film simulations.

For this reason, I do *not* recommend using GRAIN EFFECT in concert with the ACROS film simulations—it would mix the different grain effects. After all, ACROS already brings its own ISO-dependent grain to the table.

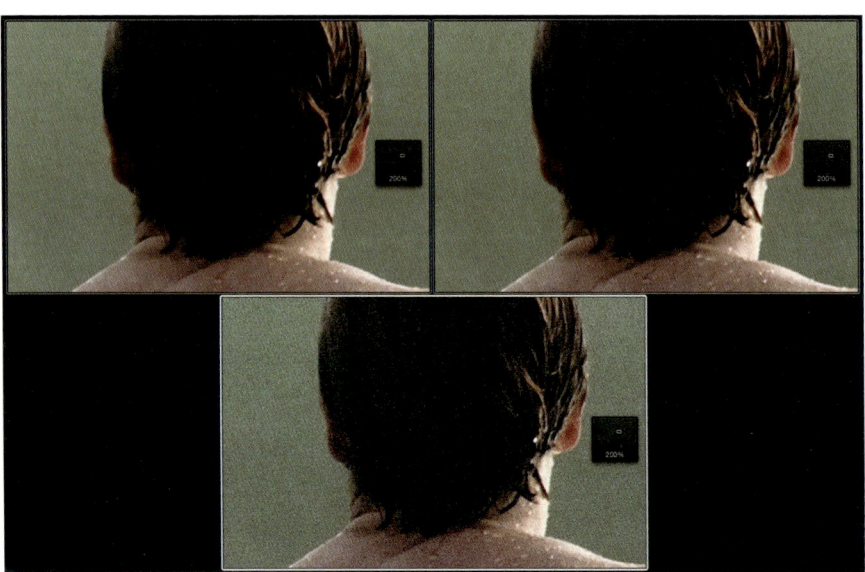

Fig. 56: GRAIN EFFECT adds natural-looking analog grain to all film simulations, providing more texture and micro contrast for an organic look. These zoomed-in samples show the same ISO 800 image without grain effect and minimal noise reduction (upper left), with a WEAK grain effect and minimal noise reduction (upper right), and with a STRONG grain effect and minimal noise reduction (center below).

The processor of the X-T2 is able to make noise look nice, so adding artificial grain may not be necessary for shots that were taken with ISO settings of 800 or higher. Instead, reduce the NOISE REDUCTION to −4 to preserve as much noise (and detail) as possible and allow the camera to do its magic.

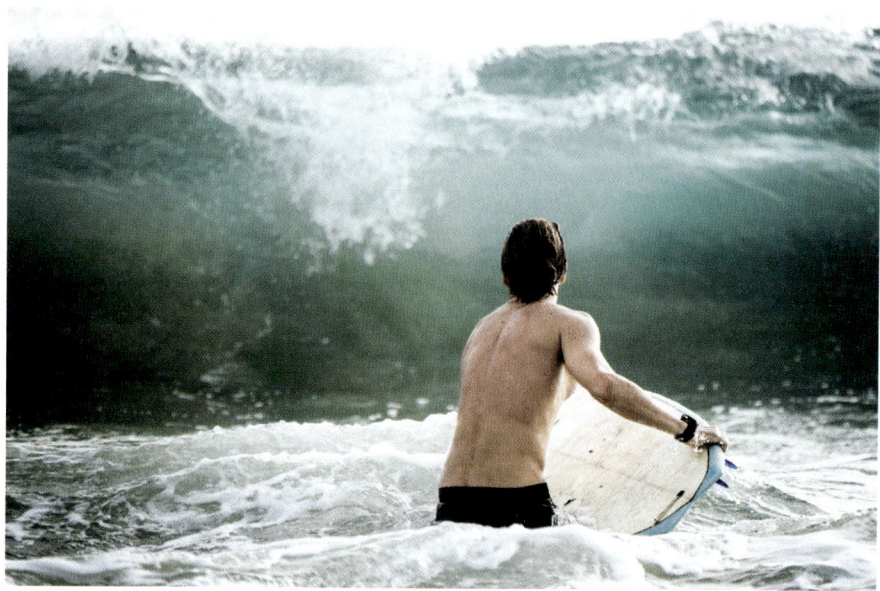

Fig. 57: Different grain effects are also available in external RAW converters and effect software. This image shows a Lightroom-processed version of our sample that includes a subtle grain effect. Adding artificial grain is about adding subtle texture and micro contrast to an image—not about noticing individual grain spots.

Contrast settings: working with highlights and shadows	TIP 88

A useful feature of the X-series is its ability to independently set the contrast [52] for dark and bright parts of a JPEG image using the HIGHLIGHT TONE and SHADOW TONE settings. These settings can also be used to extend or reduce a JPEG's dynamic range by lifting dark shadows or darkening bright highlights. To increase the overall contrast of a shot, you can increase both parameters in tandem by choosing a setting on the plus side (+1 to +4). To reduce the overall contrast, pick a negative setting for both parameters (−1 to −2).

It's worth mentioning that increased contrast also enhances the impression of image sharpness and color saturation. This is important because it shows you that JPEG parameters always work in concert with each other.

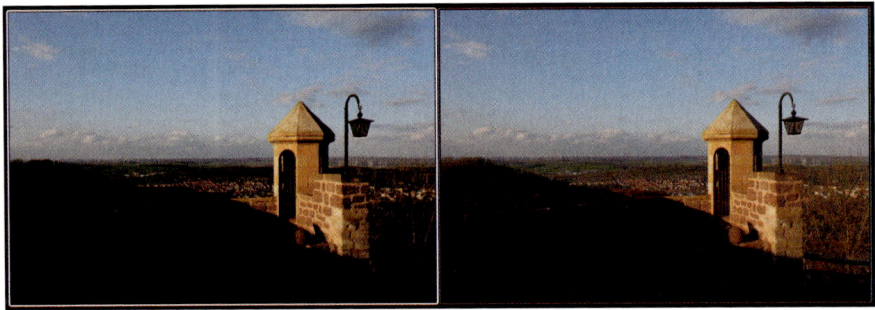

Fig. 58: Comparing **Shadow Tone** settings: The image on the left shows a SHADOW TONE +2 version; the image on the right shows the same RAW file processed with SHADOW TONE −2. As you can see, shadows and midtones are lifted up by the reduction of the JPEG's shadow contrast, while the highlights remain untouched.

TIP 89 | **Skin tones:** smooth or with texture?

The smoothness of surfaces (such as skin tones) at high ISO settings is best controlled by reducing NOISE REDUCTION. To reveal more detail and achieve less skin smoothening, you can decrease the noise reduction to −2 or lower.

If this still doesn't meet your demands, you can switch to an external RAW converter to turn RAW files into JPEGs or TIFFs. Current versions of Adobe Lightroom/ACR and Iridient Developer offer similar versions of the camera's internal film simulation modes. This means you can replicate the famous Fuji Colors and enjoy more control over many processing parameters.

Please note that RAW files recorded with extended DR settings (DR200%, DR400%) may require additional processing when you use external RAW converters. You'll have to tone-map the image and manually recover blown highlights using suitable exposure slider settings. In Lightroom and Adobe Camera Raw, you can combine the sliders for exposure, highlights, shadows, whites, and blacks to get the job done. In Iridient Developer, things are much simpler because this RAW converter offers a single Highlight Recovery slider with results that very much resemble the JPEGs from Fujifilm's internal DR function.

| Color saturation | TIP 90 |

After picking a suitable film simulation mode, you still might want to change the color saturation [53] of an image. You can do so with the COLOR setting.

Too much color saturation can obscure texture and details. For example, VELVIA is a very saturated film mode that may sometimes require a reduction in color saturation.

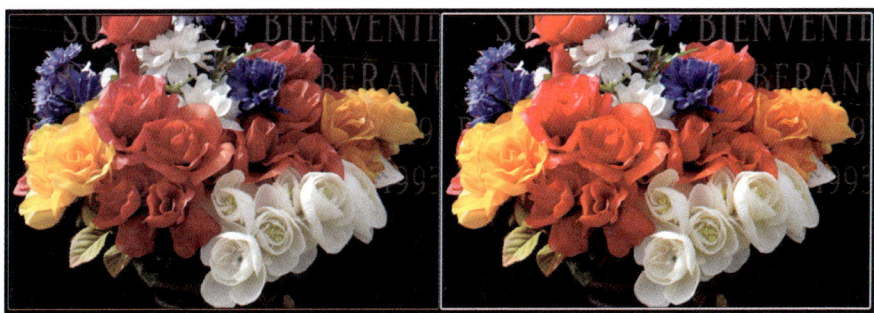

Fig. 59: **Color saturation:** The left image shows a PROVIA version with COLOR −4; the right image show the same RAW file processed with COLOR +4.

TIP 91	Choosing a color space: sRGB or Adobe RGB?

A color space [54] is a way of organizing available colors. Your X-T2 offers two options: sRGB [55] and Adobe RGB [56]. Both of these color spaces contain the same *number* of colors, but not the *same* colors—their gamuts [57] are different.

Adobe RGB covers a larger gamut than sRGB because its colors are optimized for CMYK printing. On the other hand, sRGB is optimized for computer monitors and all kinds of high-resolution displays, such as HDTVs, smartphones, and tablets. Since Adobe RGB encompasses a wider gamut than sRGB, the gaps between neighboring colors and tones are wider because both color spaces contain the same number of colors. Adobe RGB has to spread this number over its larger gamut. This larger gamut (compared to standard sRGB) is why Adobe RGB is also known as an extended color space.

Users often misunderstand and assume that "extended" means "better." It does not. The additional colors in Adobe RGB are only useful if you intend to print images with a commercial CMYK printer. This requires a calibrated workflow and a wide-gamut monitor that is capable of displaying the Adobe RGB gamut, but the majority of computer monitors are only capable of displaying the sRGB gamut. Using Adobe RGB on such a monitor would be like working with closed eyes because you wouldn't be able to see many of the colors you are using.

For most users (including me), sRGB is the best choice of color space. Images rendered in this color space can be viewed, processed, and printed on a wide variety of devices without unpleasant surprises. In any case, you should calibrate your computer monitor with hardware like Spyder. Uncalibrated screens will not give you an accurate representation of the colors in your images.

Using **custom settings** (usage profiles)	TIP 92

As you know, the X-T2 offers seven custom settings (or usage profiles) that can hold full sets of camera settings for quick access. The available settings are:

- Dynamic range
- Film simulation
- Grain effect
- White balance
- Highlight tone
- Shadow tone
- Color
- Sharpness
- Noise reduction

I'm sure you have noticed that these are the usual JPEG parameters with the addition of dynamic range.

The seven available custom settings (C1 to C7) or usage profiles aren't camera modes. They are storage spaces for seven sets of settings than can be quickly retrieved (usually via the Quick menu) to replace the currently active camera settings. Custom settings are mere shortcuts, a simple time-saver that allows you to quickly change all your camera's current settings at once instead of changing parameters one by one.

The best way to use custom settings is via the Quick menu:

- Pull up the Quick menu by pressing the Q button and select one of the seven available custom settings (C1 to C7).

- At this point, you can make changes to individual items of the retrieved parameter set using the Quick menu. Once you change a parameter, it is marked with a red dot.

- When you are happy with your settings and changes, you can make them your new current settings by pressing the OK button or by half-pressing the shutter button. In the upper-left section of the Quick menu, the currently active settings are always marked with the word BASE. You'll also see the custom setting that was last retrieved; for example, C1.

What kind of custom settings may be useful? Here are a few suggestions:

- Make sure to save your favorite all-purpose default settings in one of the seven user profiles (such as C1). This enables you to quickly revert to your default settings.

- RAW shooters can use a RAW shooter profile with dynamic range set to DR100%, HIGHLIGHT TONE −2, SHADOW TONE −2, and PRO NEG. STD film simulation.

- You could create profiles for black-and-white or infrared shooting. For example, a black-and-white profile could contain one of the eight B&W film simulations, minimal noise reduction, and additional highlight and shadow contrast.

To quickly edit custom settings, pull up the Quick menu, then press and hold the Q button again until the editing menu appears.

TIP 93	Working with the built-in RAW converter

The RAW converter in your X-T2 serves two main purposes:

- You can create different versions of a shot; for example, a colorful Velvia version and a gritty black-and-white version of the same image. Not sure what's best or what you want? Quickly create multiple versions with different film simulations and varying JPEG parameters, then sort them out later at home on your calibrated computer screen.

- You can improve your JPEGs after the fact. Since it's hard (if not impossible) to guess and set the perfect JPEG settings for each shot in advance, it's more convenient to adjust these parameters after the fact when you have time to look at your results. There's a good chance that you may be happy with many of your images. If not, you can easily make adjustments to things like white balance, color saturation, contrast settings, sharpness, or noise reduction. You can also adjust the exposure and try different film simulations.

Here are a few things you can accomplish with the built-in RAW converter:

- Use PUSH/PULL processing to brighten (push) underexposed shots or darken (pull) overexposed images.

- Use the contrast settings (SHADOW TONE and HIGH-LIGHT TONE) to selectively adjust the contrast of dark or bright parts of your image. It's perfectly adequate to combine these functions with PUSH/PULL processing. To generate JPEGs with maximum dynamic range for further post-processing on your computer, it may be useful to set both contrast parameters (shadows and highlights) to −2 and use a neutral film simulation like PRO NEG. STD.

- Adjust the color saturation of your JPEGs with the COLOR parameter. Reducing the color saturation can recover texture when one or more of the color channels appear oversaturated.

- Use SHARPNESS and NOISE REDUCTION in opposition with each other: increase sharpness while diminishing noise reduction to obtain more texture in high-ISO shots.

- Adjust the white balance using one of the presets or a Kelvin value to make your shot look warmer or cooler. Use WB SHIFT to correct or introduce a color tint.

- Want to know what the Lens Modulation Optimizer (LMO) is actually doing? Take a RAW sample and process JPEGs with and without LMO in the internal RAW converter. Then, compare the results on a computer screen. Happy pixel peeping!

- Picked the wrong color space? No problem! Just reprocess the shot with the right color space.

To process RAW files in your X-T2 that aren't stored on an SD card, you have to copy them back to a card and place them in the appropriate directory. If you are using a freshly formatted card, make sure to take at least one shot in order to create the X-T2's directory structure.

The directory where you must place your RAW files is located in a folder called DCIM. It's named "xxx-FUJI," with "xxx" being a 3-digit number that reflects the overall number of shots you have already taken. An example would be 104-FUJI.

Please remember that file transfers to the camera aren't available via USB, so make sure to insert the SD card directly into your computer or use a card reader.

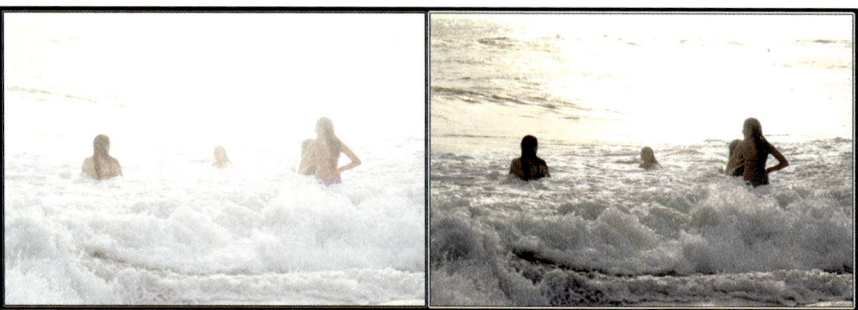

Fig. 60: The **built-in RAW converter** in action: The left image shows an overexposed sample shot that was recorded with the camera's default settings and DR400%. On the right, you can see the same shot processed with a PULL of −2 EV, maximized shadow contrast (SHADOW TONE +4), and VELVIA film simulation.

By the way, your X-T2 cannot process RAW files from other camera models, including other X-series models. However, you can process RAW files from other X-T2 cameras. In this case, your camera will display a parcel symbol indicating that the RAW file was created with a different X-T2.

Comparing RAW converters	TIP 94

So far, we have talked a lot about the X-T2's built-in RAW converter. It's the perfect tool to create JPEGs. It's a JPEG shooter's paradise! It's also super-easy, because the built-in RAW converter utilizes the same functions and parameters available in the shooting menu. That's no surprise, because the built-in RAW converter *is* the JPEG engine of the camera! If you are a JPEG shooter, ignoring the internal converter that turns RAW files to in-camera JPEGs means overlooking the aspects of the camera that make the X-T2 so special. That's why even diehard JPEG fans should shoot with FINE+RAW. You need the RAW files to feed the engine that generates JPEGs with the colors, tonality, and overall look that you like from your Fuji camera.

What about the other half—diehard RAW shooters who don't care much about JPEGs, Fuji colors, or in-camera conversion? Those guys (I tend to be one of them from time to time) require an external RAW converter to process the RAW files on a computer. The results are often saved as uncompressed 16-bit TIFF files of more than 100MB each. Such files can be further processed in Photoshop and similar applications.

In this tip, I'll compare how certain popular external RAW processors handle specific features of the X-T2:

■ **RAW File Converter EX** came free with your camera (have a look at the CD). This software is based on an older version of the Japanese Silkypix [58] RAW processor that is currently available in version 7. If you want to use all the features of this software, you should definitely upgrade to the latest version of Silkypix. As a Fujifilm camera user, you are eligible for an upgrade discount in many territories. Please note that the new RAW File Converter EX *version 2* also supports Fujifilm's film simulation modes. This software is available as a free download [59].

- The most popular RAW converter is **Adobe Lightroom**. Its processing module is also available in Photoshop as **Adobe Camera Raw**. This website [60] will provide more information and a free trial version.

- **Capture One Pro** is similar to Lightroom and deeply rooted in the professional community. It's made by PhaseOne [61], the same folks who are building medium format cameras and digital camera backs.

- A great RAW processor for macOS users is **Iridient Developer** from Iridient Digital [62]. Like Lightroom/ACR, this converter features profiles that match Fuji's built-in film simulation modes.

- **Photo Ninja** from PictureCode [63] is another fine option. Like Iridient Developer, it is able to extract a great amount of sharpness and detail from Fuji's X-Trans RAWs. It also contains a module for adaptive tone-mapping and features a special algorithm to restore blown highlights.

Which RAW converter is right for you? I don't know! But I do know that you can download free trial versions of all mentioned programs to find out for yourself. That said, it can be helpful to make a quick comparison that tells you how well specific Fuji features are supported by each software.

Those features are:

- Original Fujifilm film simulations

- Exposures taken with extended DR settings (DR200%, DR400%)

- Digital lens corrections (distortion, vignetting, etc.)

Let's have a look...

FUJIFILM FILM SIMULATIONS

Provia, Astia, Velvia, Classic Chrome, Pro Neg. Hi, and Pro Neg. Std make up the color backbone of the X-T2. Together, they constitute the Fuji Colors. However, the makers of external third-party RAW converters often have their own ideas about the look of Fuji RAWs. Your mileage may vary, as they say.

The **built-in RAW converter** is the benchmark reference for external RAW converters when it comes to emulating Fuji Colors.

- **RAW File Converter EX** and **Silkypix** feature a healthy amount of film emulations, but they all look different from Fuji's film modes. However, the new version 2 of the free RAW File Converter EX software *does* support Fuji's own film simulation modes for the X-T2, and these film simulations are also available in the commercially sold Silkypix 7.

- **Adobe Lightroom** and **Adobe Camera Raw** feature camera profiles that closely emulate Fuji's film simulation modes—as long as you are shooting in DR100% mode.

- **Capture One Pro** doesn't officially support Fuji's film modes, but it offers users the opportunity to create their own profiles. A few users have taken up the challenge, so you may find free film mode profiles in Fuji-related camera forums and blogs.

- **Iridient Developer** offers full support for Fuji's film simulation modes, but hasn't yet provided new files that are optimized for the new X-Trans III sensor. However, even the current simulation files work with the X-T2.

- **Photo Ninja** doesn't support Fuji's film modes, yet.

EXTENDED DYNAMIC RANGE (DR200%, DR400%)

Using the DR function results in RAW files that are initially exposed 1 EV (DR200%) or 2 EV (DR400%) lower than normal in order to protect critical highlights. The darker exposure is compensated during RAW conversion by a partial ISO push of the same amount that only affects shadows and midtones.

- The **built-in RAW converter** is the benchmark here, since it fully automates the tone-mapping process of partially pushing the shadows and midtones back to where they belong.

- **Silkypix** and **RAW File Converter EX** are smart citizens, too: they recognize RAW files with DR200% and DR400%, and they push them up by 1 or 2 EV, then automatically recover the blown highlights by adjusting the highlight recovery slider accordingly. That said, the results don't necessarily look exactly like the JPEGs from the camera.

- **Lightroom** and **Adobe Camera Raw** are also smart enough to recognize RAWs with extended DR settings, and they automatically push the RAWs up 1 or 2 EVs when the images are opened with the software. However, recovering the highlights isn't an automated process; it's the user's job. Sadly, this can become pretty tedious because Lightroom's exposure-related sliders work in a different way than Fuji's tone-mapping. Even worse, DR200% isn't recognized if the shot was taken in DR-Auto mode. This means that the image will look underexposed by 1 EV after importing it. To see the image with its correct brightness, you have to move the exposure slider one stop to the right. Hopefully this bug—which equally affects the X-Pro2—will have been fixed by the time you read this.

- **Capture One Pro** works just like Lightroom and applies a push of 1 or 2 EVs to RAWs that were recorded with a DR200% or DR400% setting. There's also a slider to recover highlights that may have disappeared during this push, but the results look different from Fuji's own DR tone-mapping.

- **Iridient Developer** operates like Capture One, automatically pushing RAW files that were recorded with a DR200% or DR400% setting. There's also a Highlight Recovery slider to restore highlights that may have vanished, and here's the good news: the results very much resemble the look from the camera's internal RAW converter. Well done!

- **Photo Ninja** uses its own powerful adaptive tone-mapping module, and hence doesn't really bother emulating Fuji's simple tone-mapping. There are several sliders to adjust a RAW file's exposure during processing.

DIGITAL LENS CORRECTIONS

Digital lens corrections affect four areas: de-vignetting, distortion correction, removal of chromatic aberrations (CAs), and the Lens Modulation Optimizer (LMO). The information to perform such corrections is stored in the metadata of each RAW file. Every RAW converter can potentially read and use this metadata to apply appropriate image corrections. However, not all programs are able to do so.

- The **built-in RAW converter** supports all four types of lens correction. Note that most of Fuji's high-end prime lenses (like the XF14mmF2.8, XF23mmF1.4, XF35mmF1.4, and XF56mmF1.2) don't require digital distortion correction because they are already fully optically corrected. The LMO is only available in concert with XF lenses. XC lenses and Zeiss Touit lenses don't support the LMO.

- **Silkypix** and **RAW File Converter EX** can read and process the RAW metadata for distortion correction, de-vignetting, and CAs. All corrections are automatically applied and can't be controlled by the user. There is no LMO support.

- **Lightroom** and **Adobe Camera Raw** can also process lens-correction metadata and automatically apply the respective corrections in the background. It's currently not possible to control or stop the application of these lens corrections. However, it is possible to employ user-defined correction profiles that can be applied *in addition* to the automatic metadata application. It is not possible to *replace* metadata with user-defined corrections. There is no LMO support.

- **Capture One Pro** can also process lens-correction metadata. Unlike Lightroom and Silkypix, it allows the user to control the intensity of the corrections or switch them off altogether. There is no LMO support.

- **Iridient Developer** can use lens-correction metadata, too. Like Capture One, it also provides control over the extent of the corrections. There is no LMO support.

- **Photo Ninja** ignores all lens-correction metadata. Instead, the software asks the user to provide suitable profiles or to manually correct distortion, vignetting, and CAs.

Automatic lens metadata corrections can look a bit different depending on the RAW converter because each converter tends to interpret the data differently.

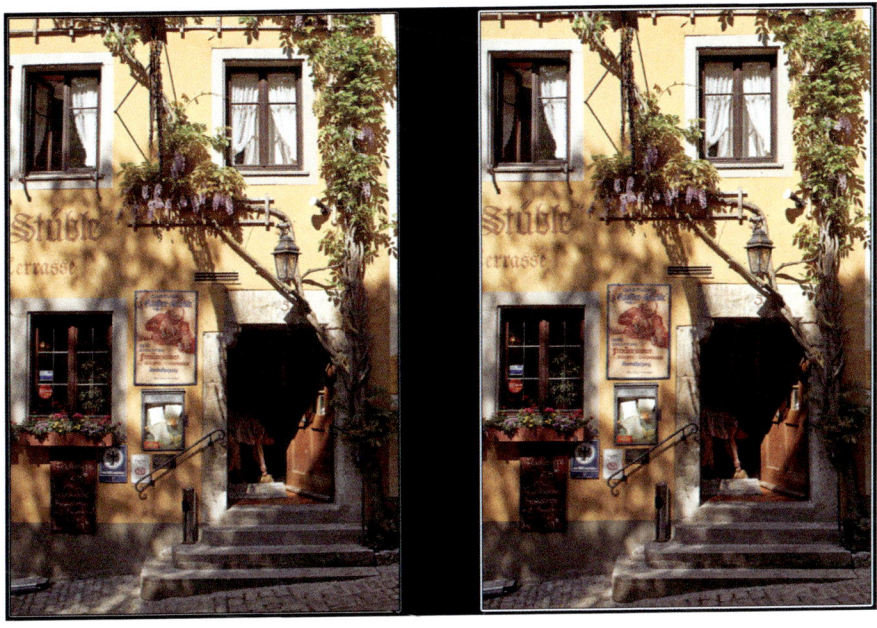

Fig. 61: **Digital lens correction:** This shot was taken with a Zeiss Touit 1.8/32 lens. The left image shows the shot without digital distortion correction. On the right, you can see how the RAW converter applied the digital distortion correction to straighten the lines.

Important: At the time of delivering this manuscript, Capture One Pro was still unable to deal with compressed RAW files from the X-Pro2 and X-T2.

Displaying EXIF metadata	TIP 95

Digital cameras save information about every recorded image in the EXIF [21] data of each RAW or JPEG file. This data can be useful to RAW converters and cataloging software, but it can also be useful to you to help you understand how an image was exposed.

EXIF data consists of information about exposure parameters, camera settings, date and time, focal length, AF settings, white balance, JPEG parameters, DR mode, digital lens correction data, serial numbers of cameras and lenses, etc. Many of these data points are saved in an area called "maker notes," which contains information on camera features that are specific to a certain brand (like Fujifilm). ExifTool can read the EXIF data and is also able to make sense of maker notes. ExifTool is rarely stand-alone. Instead, you can get it as part of other image utilities, such as ExifTool GUI for Windows or GraphicConverter for macOS users.

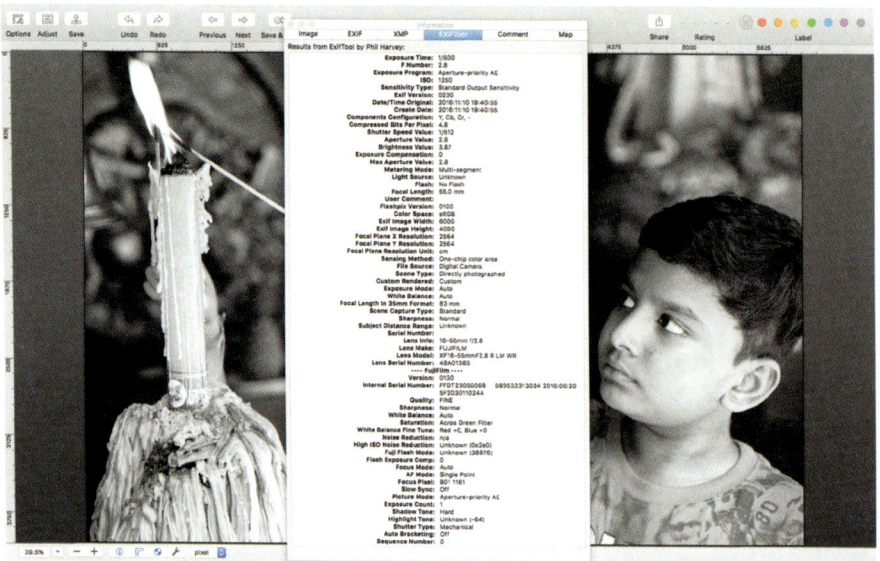

Fig. 62: **EXIF** data of an X-T2 shot in GraphicConverter: There's a vast amount of information about every image, including brand-specific Fujifilm maker notes.

2.6 BURST MODE, MOVIES, MOTION PANORAMA, AND THE SELF TIMER

The DRIVE dial of your X-T2 gives access to several modes and functions that control bracketing options, burst shooting, panorama mode, etc.

Some of the bracketing options are only available in JPEG mode, so those of us who shoot FINE+RAW will never use them:

■ Film simulation bracketing
■ ISO bracketing
■ DR bracketing
■ White balance bracketing

Due to technical reasons, Advanced Filters and Multiple Exposure modes don't save RAW files, either:

■ MULTIPLE EXPOSURE is actually just a double exposure. It's a simple feature that merges two consecutively taken JPEGs. Usually, it's better to perform this in software like Photoshop.

■ ADVANCED FILTER offers a variety of special effects. Most of them are gimmicks, but give them a try and see what they can do for you!

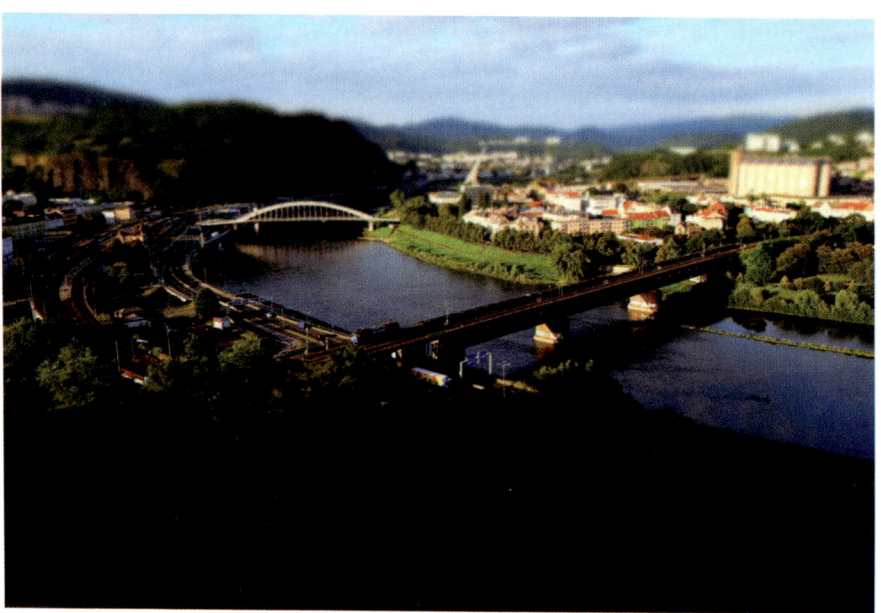

Fig. 63: MINIATURE is a popular filter that turns cityscapes into tiny model towns.

Using **burst mode**

In burst or Continuous mode, the camera takes a quick sequence of shots while you press and hold the shutter button. The X-T2 offers two basic speed settings: CL (3 fps, 4 fps, or 5 fps) and CH (8 fps, 11 fps with the optional Vertical Power Booster Grip, or even up to 14 fps with the electronic shutter). In principle, both speed settings work in the same way:

- White balance, autofocus, DR settings, and exposure (aperture, shutter speed, ISO) are determined for the first frame of the series and then carried over to all consecutive shots. This means that all shots of the series have the same white balance, autofocus, DR settings, and exposure.

■ As usual, there's one exception: using AF-C in concert with burst shooting, the camera will refocus (track) before each frame. If SHUTTER AE is set to OFF, it will also adjust the exposure of each shot. However, white balance and DR settings are still carried over from the first frame of the series.

Shooting **motion panoramas**	TIP 97

MOTION PANORAMA is a derivate of burst mode: while you pan the camera in a horizontal or vertical motion, the X-T2 takes a series of images and stitches them together in a panoramic JPEG file. You can choose between two sizes (M and L), and you can specify the direction of your panning motion (left, right, up, and down).

You can use a vertical motion horizontally by holding the camera upright. This results in a maximum image size of 9600×2160 pixels for a size L motion panorama.

Here are a few tips for getting the best results with motion panoramas:

■ Since MOTION PANORAMA results in only a JPEG file (no RAW), JPEG parameters such as white balance and film simulation have to be set *before* taking the shots.

■ White balance and focusing remain constant during the recording of a motion panorama. This applies to all focus modes (AF-S, AF-C, and MF). That's why it's important to set a focus distance and depth of field that work for the entire panoramic scene.

■ Panoramas tend to extend over a wide area with varying light conditions and strong changes in contrast. In such cases, it's smart to shoot with an extended DR setting, such as DR200% or DR400%. In addition to that, the exposure should be set in a way that suits the entire panoramic image, not just a small part of it. The edges of a panorama are rarely representative; it's usually better to base your exposure on the main part of the image in the middle. Motion panorama works with all four exposure modes, so shooting it in manual mode **M** may be the smartest option. Please note that motion panorama only works with multi metering.

- If you decide to *not* manually set exposure, white balance, and focus, point the camera towards a representative part of the panoramic scene, then lock focus, exposure, white balance, and DR by half-pressing the shutter button. Then pan to the point where you'd like to start the panning action (while holding the shutter button half-depressed), press the shutter button fully, and start panning. Don't forget that SHUTTER AE must be set to ON to lock the exposure of the panorama by half-pressing the shutter.

- Avoid scenes that contain a lot of motion. Moving objects (people, vehicles, etc.) can lead to ghosting artifacts, which is when moving objects (partially) appear in more than one spot of the final panorama.

- Keep a healthy distance to the panoramic scene. Don't shoot panoramas in close quarters. Also make sure that you have sufficient depth of field. Wide-angle lenses are better suited for this job than normal or telephoto lenses.

- Always pan with the EVF (camera held to your eye), not with the LCD display (arms stretched in front of you).

- While panning, stand parallel to the panoramic scene and always stand on level ground.

- Try to ignore the time delay that may occur between the currently recorded image and what's displayed in the EVF. Keep panning the camera in a smooth motion until the camera stops taking frames.

- Banding in the final JPEG can indicate that the shutter speed was too fast. In this case, try again with a slower shutter speed.

- Use a tripod and make sure the camera is leveled to the horizon.

- Immediately check your finished panorama in the camera's viewfinder after you have captured it. Look out for stitching errors and ghosting artifacts. Do this while you are still on location, not at home when it's too late to reshoot a panorama that went wrong.

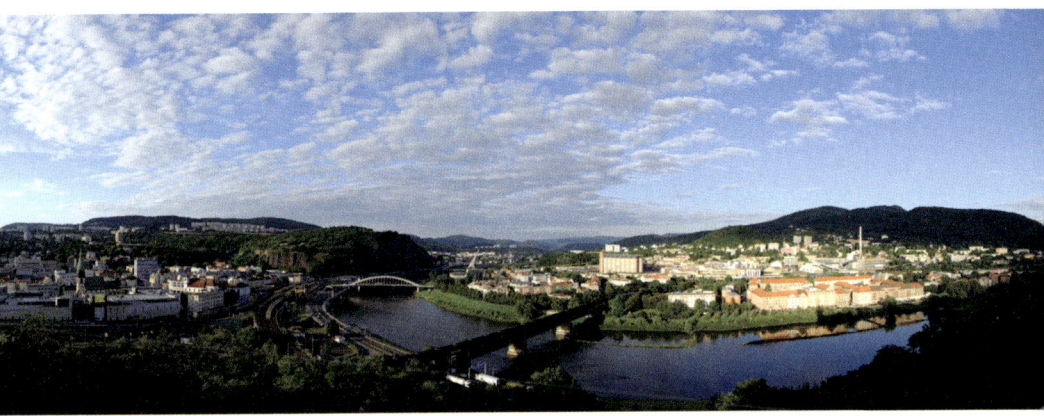

Fig. 64: A medium-sized (6400×2160) **motion panorama** using the Velvia film simulation: The camera automatically takes as many frames as it needs to stitch the panoramic JPEG image.

Shooting video with the X-T2	TIP 98

After setting the DRIVE dial to MOVIE mode, pressing the shutter button will commence video recording in HD or 4K quality. In the MOVIE SETTING menu, you can choose between several resolutions and frame rates, set an auto-focus mode (AREA or MULTI), or select a target medium for your output. Since video is still a work in progress and a new priority for Fujifilm, you can expect future firmware updates with improvements and new features down the road. On my website, Fuji X Secrets [64], I will publish updates covering significant X-T2 firmware releases, so please visit this site regularly if you do not want to miss important updates to this book.

The following notes are based on X-T2 firmware 1.10, which was released in November 2016:

- MOVIE mode is available in concert with all four **exposure modes** (**P**, **A**, **S**, **M**), so you can change both aperture and shutter speed *before* and *during* recording. However, you can't change the exposure mode during a recording. There's also full manual ISO control between ISO 200 and ISO 12800 *before* you start recording. Auto-ISO is supported, too. In this case, the camera will automatically select ISO settings between 200 and 12800 (actually, it may even be a little bit higher than 12800). Your Auto-ISO configuration for still photography (default sensitivity, max. sensitivity, min. shutter speed) is ignored in video mode. Please note that the shutter speed can never be slower than the selected frame rate. For example, at 60fps, the shutter speed has to be 1/60s or faster.

- The only **exposure metering** mode available in video mode is multi metering. In modes **P**, **A**, and **S**, the camera automatically adjusts the exposure during video recording. However, you can bias the exposure with the camera's exposure compensation dial before and during recording within a range of ±2 EV.

- **Focusing** is possible with all three modes: AF-S, AF-C, and MF. You can also switch modes during filming. AF-S sets the focus before recording starts, so there's no AF tracking during video recording. AF-C continuously adjusts the focus during video recording. If MOVIE SETTING > MOVIE AF MODE > AREA is selected, you can move the focus frame during recording with the focus stick. In MF mode, you can adjust the focus with the focus ring before or during video recording. One-Touch-AF (Instant AF) is available, but only before you start recording. Focus peaking is also available in MF mode, but you can't zoom into the image during recording. In AF-C mode, you can use the X-T2's AF-C Custom Settings to fine-tune AF-C tracking behavior for the task at hand. For example, Tracking Sensitivity defines how quickly the AF-C changes its focus towards a new target that has a significantly different distance to the camera than the previous one. Pick a low value (like 0 or 1) if you want the camera to make quick focus changes to a new target. Pick a high value (like 3 or 4) if you want the autofocus to longer stay on the previous target when it moves out of the focus frame.

■ **Face detection** is also currently only available for HD, not 4K movie modes. Face detection operates like AF-C, so it's continuously adjusting focus and exposure with respect to the detected face closest to the center of the scene. Eye detection is not supported.

■ Sadly, there is no support for the **DR function** in video mode. There also are no "zebras" or "blinkies" to mark overexposed areas. You have to trust the live view (there is no live histogram during video recording) and adjust the exposure as necessary.

■ With automatic **white balance** (AUTO), the X-T2 is continuously adjusting the white balance during video recording. You can also use one of the white balance presets or a Kelvin setting. Custom white balance is available, too.

■ You can adjust the look of your videos by selecting one of the camera's 15 **film simulations**. Contrast settings (HIGHLIGHT TONE, SHADOW TONE), color and sharpness are also adjustable for video recordings.

■ In 4K video mode, the X-T2 exhibits a **crop factor** of 1.17x.

■ Internally on an SD card, the X-T2 is recording video in the 4:2:0 format. However, you can record 4K video to an external HDMI device in the 4:2:2 format with even better quality. **External recording** also offers an "F-Log" option, which is Fujifilm's version of a flat video profile for maximum dynamic range. F-Log videos require post-processing—you can download an F-Log LUT here [65].

- In movie mode, the X-T2 also records **audio**. You can either use the built-in stereo microphone or attach an external microphone. The latter is recommended if you don't want to record camera sounds like the AF motor or aperture changes. An external microphone is available from Fujifilm, but you can of course also use third-party offerings. You can adjust the sensitivity of the audio recording with the MIC LEVEL ADJUSTMENT menu option. If you use a Vertical Power Booster Grip, there's also a headphone jack.

- Using a lens with **optical image stabilization** (OIS) reduces camera shake during video recording. Just make sure that the OIS is switched on.

- You can use the Vertical Power Booster Grip to extend the single-take shooting time of 4K videos from 10 minutes to 30 minutes.

TIP 99	Using the **self-timer**

The camera's built-in self-timer delays the shutter release (exposure) after you press the shutter button. This function isn't available on the DRIVE dial; you have to find it in the SHOOTING SETTING menu (or the Quick menu). You can select one of two delay options:

- A 10-second delay is typically used when you want to make sure that you are also in the picture when the shot is taken. Press the shutter button and run.

- A 2-second delay replaces a remote shutter release when you are working on a tripod. The delay helps the camera to settle down, so there's no camera shake or vibration when the actual exposure begins.

2.7 FLASH PHOTOGRAPHY

Flash photography means taking a double exposure. A flash shot always consists of two components that are merged into one: **surrounding light** and **flash light**.

■ The **surrounding-light** component is metered like a regular exposure. The camera is metering the scene with multi, average, center-weighted, or spot metering, while the exposure mode (**P**, **A**, or **S**) automatically selects suitable exposure parameters based on your adjustment of the exposure compensation dial. As usual, the live view and live histogram are your friends. You can also set the exposure of the surrounding light component manually in mode **M**. Basically, exposing the surrounding-light component works exactly like exposing a scene without flash.

■ The **flash-light** component is automatically metered and adjusted by the camera to match the overall exposure. To accomplish this, the X-T2 employs a so-called TTL metering system. TTL stands for Through The Lens. It means that the flash light is entering the camera through the lens before it's metered with the image sensor. This happens with the help of a weaker pre-flash that is emitted solely for metering purposes. You can bias the strength of the automatic flash-light component either on the FLASH FUNCTION SETTING page, or directly on external Fujifilm TTL flash units like the EF-X20. Please note that while the live view and live histogram provide a preview of the surrounding-light component, they completely ignore the flash-light component that will be added to the final image.

Besides Fuji and Fuji-compatible TTL flash units, you can also use generic third-party flash units. Pretty much everything that fits onto the hot shoe works. Using generic third-party flash units means that TTL flash metering [66] is no longer available, so you must manually set the flash energy output. You can also use automatic flash units that use their own built-in light sensor to automatically measure and adjust the flash output.

The TTL flash logic in your X-T2 supports several flash modes that can be selected in the Quick menu or on the FLASH SETTING > FLASH FUNCTION SETTING page:

- TTL AUTO is only available in mode **P** and automatically fires an available flash unit if the camera decides it's necessary. It's a silly mode, since you probably know better than your camera whether or not you want to use a flashgun. When the flash is firing, it works just like regular TTL, which is our next mode.

- TTL STANDARD (formerly known as FORCED FLASH) always fires an active flash unit. This setting is available in all of the four exposure modes (**P**, **A**, **S**, and **M**).

- TTL SLOW SYNC works like standard TTL, but allows shutter speeds as long as 1/8s to better capture the surrounding-light component. This can be helpful when the light is poor and you still want to capture more of the background. This setting is only available in modes **P** and **A**.

- MANUAL FLASH works like TTL SLOW SYNC, but allows you to manually specify the light emission power. This setting is available in all four exposure modes (**P**, **A**, **S**, and **M**).

- COMMANDER is a trigger flash that optically releases other external flash units (or slaves) that feature an optical sensor. This function is available in Fuji's EF-X20 and several third-party flash units. Please note that you have to manually adjust the power of the triggered slave flash. Don't forget that the commander flash is also emitting flash light that can affect the exposure of your scene, especially when you are shooting with high ISO settings. Commander is available in all four exposure modes (**P**, **A**, **S**, and **M**).

■ SUPPRESSED FLASH makes sure that no flash is fired, even when the flash is switched on and connected to the camera.

■ In the FLASH FUNCTION SETTING page, there is an option to specify whether the flash is supposed to fire on the FRONT (1st) or REAR (2nd) curtain. This option is available in all flash modes, and it is relevant for shooting moving subjects at slow shutter speeds. Since flash photography is a double exposure, it makes a difference whether the flash is fired at the beginning or at the end of a longer exposure. With the new EF-X500 flashgun, there's also an option called FP, which stands for Focal Plane. This is Fuji's version of HSS, a.k.a. High Speed Synchronization, which allows firing the flash at all shutter speeds up to 1/8000s.

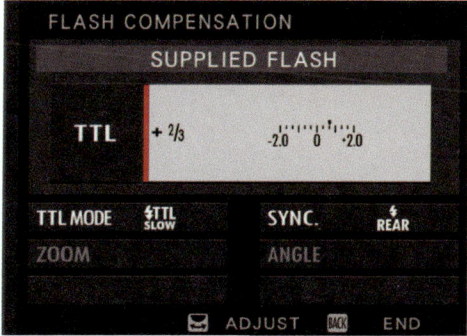

Fig. 65: The FLASH FUNCTION SETTING PAGE lets you control flash parameters such as flash mode, sync. Mode, and flash exposure compensation.

TIP 100 **Flash photography in modes P and A**: slow shutter speed limits

In exposure modes P and A, the camera automatically selects suitable shutter speeds to capture the surrounding-light component of the scene.

- In flash modes TTL AUTO, TTL STANDARD, and COMMANDER, the slowest available shutter speed is approximately the reciprocal of the focal length divided by 2. For example, shooting with a 55mm focal length, the slowest available shutter speed will be 1/55s/2 = 1/110s. This is a hard limit. Another hard limit in these modes is 1/30s. No matter what focal length is in use, the camera will not use a slower shutter speed than that. These hard limits mark the point where the surrounding-light component (basically the background) of the shot can end up underexposed. There are exceptions, though. *Exception number 1:* Lenses with built-in and active OIS ignore the reciprocal rule and only follow the hard minimal shutter speed limit of 1/30s. *Exception number 2:* Auto-ISO can overrule both shutter speed limits for flash photography (the reciprocal limit and the 1/30s minimum) if you set a slower minimum shutter speed in Auto-ISO, such as 1/15, 1/8, or 1/4s. To achieve even slower shutter speeds in concert with flash photography, you should use mode S or M.

- TTL SLOW SYNC and MANUAL FLASH allow the camera to use slower minimum shutter speeds with flash photography. There's only one hard limit of 1/8s, which is independent from the focal length or an active OIS. To achieve even slower shutter speeds, you should use mode S or M.

Controlling the surrounding-light component of flash pho- **TIP 101**
tography

When you are metering a scene with your X-T2, you will quickly realize that it doesn't make any difference whether the flash is turned on or off while doing so. The metering result will always be the same. In other words, the X-T2 is always metering the surrounding-light component in the same way, with or without flash. In case you choose to use a flash, the flash-light component will simply be *added* to the surrounding-light component.

This is important because it tells us that we don't have to fear some camera voodoo that may or may not influence the metering of the surrounding light as soon as we switch on a flash. Instead, we can be certain that the camera's metering will always deliver consistent results. This also means that it's our job to balance both light components, for example by reducing the surrounding-light components to make room for more flash light in the composite exposure.

Typically, if you want to use the flash as a fill-in light to brighten a dark foreground (such as a backlit person), you wouldn't have to change much, since the flash-light component would brighten the dark foreground simply by filling in the light that's missing. However, if you use the flash on a scene that's already fully exposed by natural light, the camera's TTL flash metering would come to the conclusion that no additional light is needed. The forced flash would still fire, of course, but with minimal output; it would probably be almost invisible in the resulting shot. In order to emphasize the flash-light component, reduce the exposure of the surrounding-light component.

Here's how it works:

■ You can control the exposure of the surrounding-light component either with the exposure compensation dial or by setting an appropriate manual exposure (ISO, aperture, shutter speed). Less surrounding light will prompt the TTL flash metering to add a stronger flash-light component, since the TTL flash system will always try to deliver balanced results. Changing the exposure compensation dial has no effect on the flash component of the shot; it only affects the exposure of the surrounding-light component.

■ To control the surrounding-light component in manual mode **M** using the live view and the live histogram, make sure to set SET UP > SCREEN SET-UP > PREVIEW EXP./WB IN MANUAL MODE > PREVIEW EXP./WB.

■ In a studio, you often want to minimize the surrounding-light component and illuminate your subject entirely with flash light. In such cases, I recommend small aperture settings (large aperture numbers), base ISO 200, and a fast shutter speed. The fastest official flash synchronization speed of the X-T2 is 1/250s, but some flash units allow you to go a little bit faster. In order to compose a scene with very little surrounding light in mode **M**, set SET UP > SCREEN SET-UP > PREVIEW EXP./WB IN MANUAL MODE > OFF. Otherwise, it will be hard to see anything in the viewfinder other than darkness.

■ Sometime the fastest available flash sync speed (1/250s) will still overexpose the surrounding-light component, even at base ISO 200. Yes, you could stop down the aperture, but this might negate the purpose of achieving a nice subject-to-background separation with little depth of field. In such a case, it's useful to attach a neutral density filter [36] to the lens to reduce the amount of light that hits the sensor by 3 to 6 stops.

- Similar to the DR function, flash light is often used to reduce contrast between a dark subject and a bright background. You can combine both features, which may be useful if the background—when viewed isolated from the foreground—still contains so much contrast that DR expansion is required. Think of a night scene with city lights, street lamps, and bright billboards in the background. In such a scenario, a flashgun could illuminate a person standing in the foreground, while the DR function (DR400%) would help capture the colors and textures of the city lights. DR400% is also useful when you are illuminating scenes with subjects that expand deep into space and don't have an equal distance to the camera. In such cases, DR400% will give subjects that are closer to the flash-light an additional overexposure protection of 2 EV which can be retrieved during external RAW conversion of your shot.

- The previously discussed hard limits for minimum shutter speed in modes **P** and **A** can lead to an underexposed surrounding-light component. However, these limits are quite useful because they prevent shaky or blurred backgrounds in hand-held shots. This isn't an issue when using a tripod, so you could circumvent the limits by selecting TTL SLOW or by manually setting a slow shutter speed in **S** or **M** mode.

- Surrounding light and flash light frequently exhibit different color temperatures, which makes it difficult to find a white balance setting that suits all parts of the image. Luckily, some RAW converters (like Lightroom) allow selective white balance editing in an image. Another method is to use a gel filter in front of the flash unit to warm or cool the flash light to better match the surrounding light.

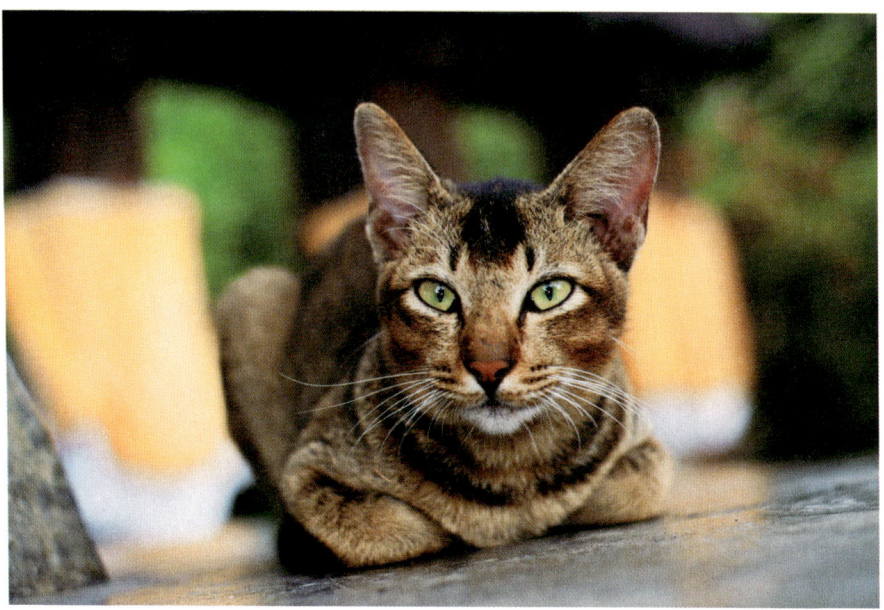

Fig. 66: With plenty of surrounding light, the flash-light component takes a backseat. In this example it simply added a spark to
the cat's eyes. The best flash shots are often those that aren't easy
to identify as flash photography.

TIP 102	Controlling the flash-light component

If the flash-light component of your image turns out too
bright or dark, you can bias the camera's TTL flash system:

- To bias the flash-light component of your shot, you can
  adjust the flash exposure compensation in the camera
  on the FLASH SETTING > FLASH FUNCTION SETTING
  page or on many external TTL flash units. Combining
  the in-camera flash compensation with an additional
  compensation setting on the flash unit itself will simply
  add up both corrections (the new EF-X500 is an exception
  to this rule).

- You will often get nicer-looking results by bouncing the
  flash off the ceiling, which makes the flash light look
  softer. Of course, bouncing the flash light requires much

more power, so you may need a stronger flash. It's also worth noting that bouncing the flash from a colored surface will tint the light accordingly.

■ To add a tint or change the color temperature of your flash light, you can attach colored gel filters in front of your reflector. The color temperature of unfiltered flash light usually corresponds to regular daylight.

■ The range of your flash unit depends on the set aperture, the ISO setting, and (of course) the power setting. In TTL mode, the camera is automatically adjusting the light output of your flash, but many flash units can also be set to manual. This way, you are the one setting the power output of the flash. In manual mode **M**, changing the shutter speed doesn't affect the brightness of the flash-light component of your shot. Hence, changing the shutter speed is a quick way to adjust the exposure of the surrounding-light component without messing with your carefully balanced manual flash-light setup.

■ Don't forget that large lenses and lens hoods can block parts of the flash, resulting in unpleasant shadows. It's better to remove the lens hood or to use off-camera flash.

■ Some wide-angle lenses cover a larger angle of view than the reflector of your flash. This results in unpleasant vignetting. In such cases, bouncing the flash light off the ceiling can be helpful. Alternatively, you can attach a diffusor to the flash reflector. Many flash units feature built-in diffusors—just don't forget to flip it on.

Rear curtain flash synchronization: what's the deal?	TIP 103

Flash photographs are double exposures consisting of surrounding light and flash light. When you shoot the surrounding light with a slow shutter speed, there is the question of when the flash (with its much faster speed) should fire. Normally, the flash is fired along with the shutter opening its FRONT curtain at the *beginning* of an exposure. However, selecting the REAR curtain makes the flash fire at the *end* of the exposure when the rear shutter curtain closes.

Naturally, moving objects change their position during the exposure of a shot. Synchronizing the flash with the rear curtain ensures that moving objects are frozen where they are at the end of the exposure as opposed to the beginning. This often results in the moving object appearing more natural in the image.

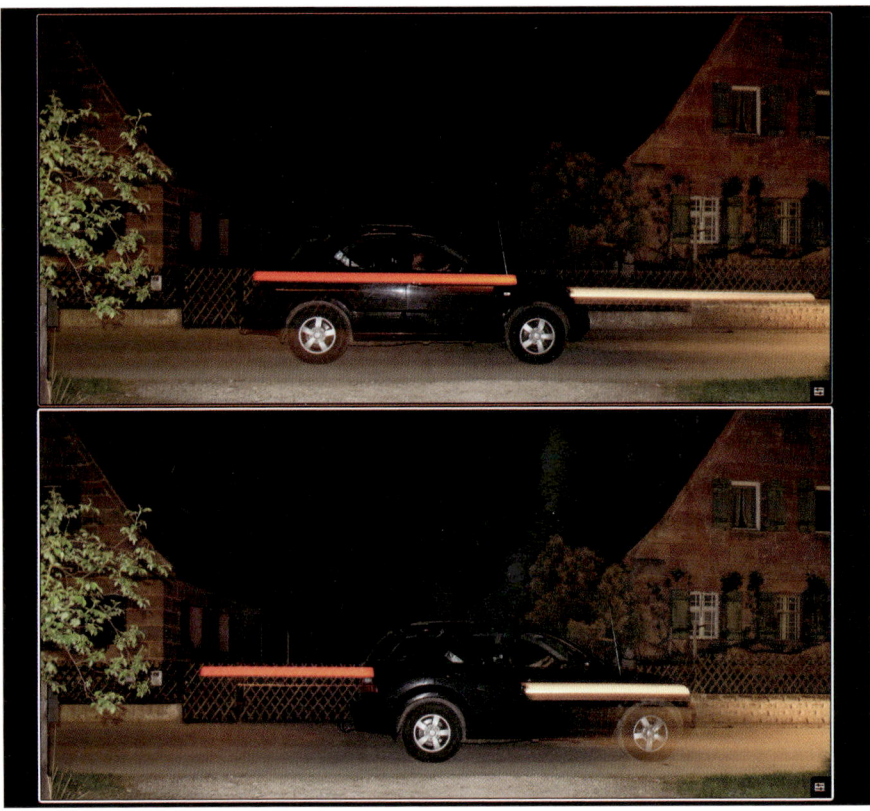

Fig. 67: Front vs. rear curtain sync: This examples shows the same scene photographed with front curtain sync (above) and rear curtain sync (below). The shot above shows how the flash freezes the moving vehicle at the beginning of the exposure while the shot below shows it being frozen at the end of the exposure. The rear-curtain version looks more natural and avoids the false impression of the car moving backward. This is also a good example to examine in terms of the nature of flash photographs as double exposures. You can see how the slow shutter speed captures the moving vehicle as a blurry trail of light, while the fast flash instantly freezes parts of it.

Flash synchronization: where's the limit?   **TIP 104**

Officially, the fastest flash sync [67] speed of the X-T2 is 1/250s.

- In exposure modes **P** and **A**, the camera will never offer a shutter speed faster than 1/250s. If this is too slow for the current light conditions, the surrounding-light component will be overexposed. In this case, the shutter speed of 1/250s will be displayed in red. To avoid overexposure, stop down the lens, reduce ISO (but never below 200), or use a neutral density (ND) [36] filter in front of the lens.

- In exposure modes **S** and **M**, you are able to select shutter speeds faster than 1/250s. The X-T2 will honor these settings in flash mode, but there will be a price to pay: the resulting images will display some partial shadowing of the flash. It's often possible to use shutter speeds that are a little bit faster than 1/250s without visible negative effects—it depends on the type of flash you are using. Its power setting plays a role, as well. Proceed at your own risk!

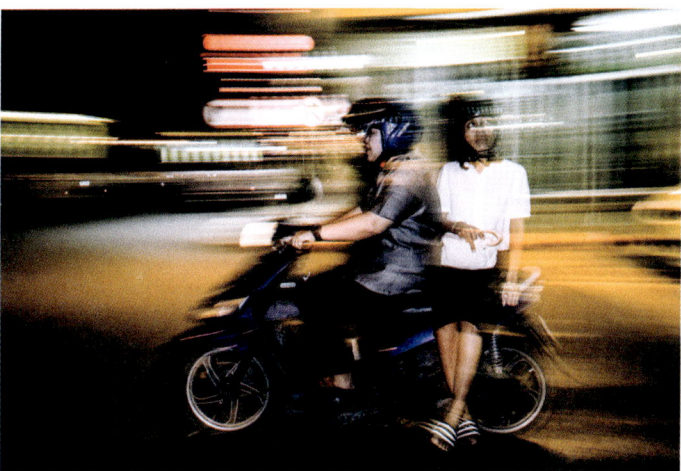

Fig. 68: Many photographers wish to use a **flash sync speed** faster than 1/250s with their X-T2. That said, it's also possible to deliberately use very slow synch speeds to create a blurry background behind a more contoured flash-lit foreground.

■ High-speed synchronization (HSS) up to 1/8000s is officially supported by the X-T2, but not available with most Fuji-TTL-compatible flashguns. As of November 2016, the only HSS-compatible flash from Fujifilm is the new EF-X500. Some Fuji-TTL-compatible third-party flashguns (Nissin, Metz, etc.) support HSS, as well, but will often require a firmware update to make it work in concert with your X-T2.

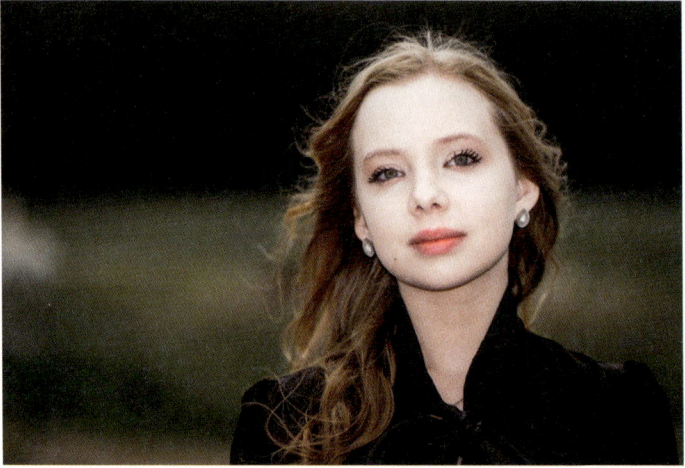

Fig. 69: This manually controlled **HSS** shot was taken with a shutter speed of 1/3200s.

| TIP 105 | **Red-eye removal:** a two-step affair |

If the flash and your subject share (almost) the same optical axis, this can lead to the red-eye effect [68]: an unpleasant red reflection in the eyes of humans or animals.

■ If you pull up FLASH SETTING > RED EYE REMOVAL and then select either FLASH (or FLASH+REMOVAL), the camera will emit a pre-flash prior to each shot that forces your subject's pupils to contract, thus reducing or eliminating the red-eye effect.

■ In addition to the pre-flash, there's *another* red-eye removal tool available: selecting REMOVAL (or FLASH+ REMOVAL) in the FLASH SETTING > RED EYE REMOVAL menu will detect and remove unpleasant red-eye effects in a JPEG after the fact. This function is also available in PLAYBACK MENU > RED EYE REMOVAL in case you decide to use it later. If you want to keep a copy of the unretouched JPEG, select SET UP > SAVE DATA SET-UP > SAVE ORG IMAGE > ON. The RAW file isn't affected by this variant of red-eye removal.

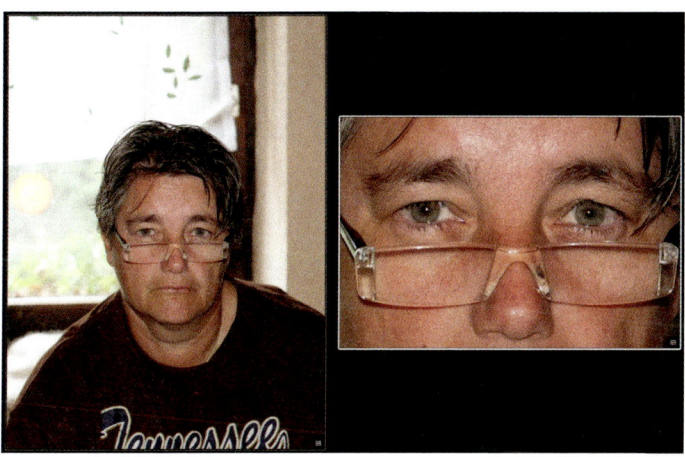

Fig. 70: The **red-eye removal** function in the X-T2 emits a pre-flash that is bright enough to prompt your subject's pupils to contract. This example shows a crop of the actual image.

Using **TTL-Lock**	TIP 106

TTL-Lock works similar to AE-Lock: Where AE-Lock locks the exposure of the surrounding-light component, TTL-Lock locks the exposure of the flash-light component. In order to use TTL-Lock, you have to first assign it to one of the X-T2's Fn buttons.

TTL-Lock can work in one of two ways:

- Lock the exposure of the most recent flash exposure when you press the TTL-Lock button (FLASH SETTING > TTL-LOCK MODE > LOCK WITH LAST FLASH).

- Meter the flash exposure with a metering flash when you press the TTL-Lock button and immediately lock the metered result (FLASH SETTING > TTL-LOCK MODE > LOCK WITH METERING FLASH).

TTL-Lock is practical in situations where you want to take more than one picture of the same scene and maintain a consistent flash output for the entire series. A typical method involves setting the LOCK WITH LAST FLASH option and taking a few test shots of the scene and applying flash exposure compensation until the result looks great. Now press TTL-Lock to lock this "perfect" flash exposure while you take additional pictures of the scene.

TIP 107	Little slave: the EF-X20

Fuji's TTL system flash EF-X20 was specifically made for retro-style cameras like the X-Pro1, but also works perfectly with your X-T2. Besides using it as a TTL flash, you can also set its output power manually. You can even trigger it wirelessly with another flash, such as the camera's Commander flash.

- Set the flash mode in your X-T2 to COMMANDER.

- Move the mode switch on your EF-X20 to the N position.

- Manually set the desired flash output on your EF-X20. There are seven levels, from 1/1 (full power) to 1/64.

With this setup, the flash on your X-T2 will wirelessly trigger the EF-X20. Please take into account that the light emitted by the commander flash can still affect your image.

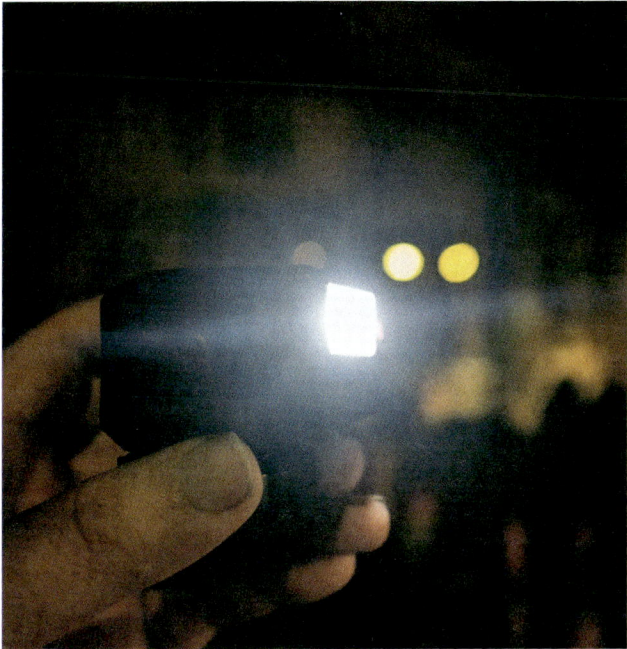

Fig. 71: An optically triggered **EF-X20** slave flash

Big master: the EF-X500	TIP 108

The EF-X500 is Fuji's version of a professional flashgun, with wireless TTL control of several flash units (organized in up to three independent groups), stroboscope flash, and a secondary LED reflector that can be used as a catchlight [69], a more powerful AF assist lamp or a video lamp. It also features FP high-speed sync to support shutter speeds of up to 1/8000s.

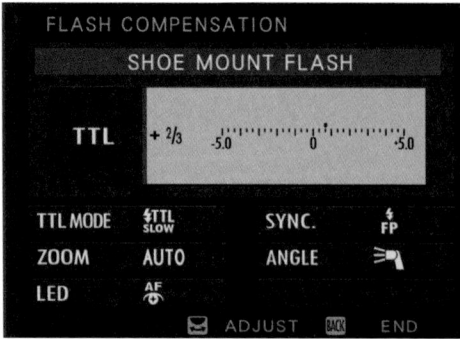

Fig. 72: With the fully featured **EF-X500** attached, the FLASH FUNCTION SETTING page adds several new items, including high-speed sync (FP), zoom settings, a reflector angle control, and control of the secondary LED, which can be used as an AF assist lamp and/or a catchlight.

You can use the EF-X500 as a single flashgun or as a master/ slave in setups with multiple wireless flash units. Communication between master and slave units is light based.

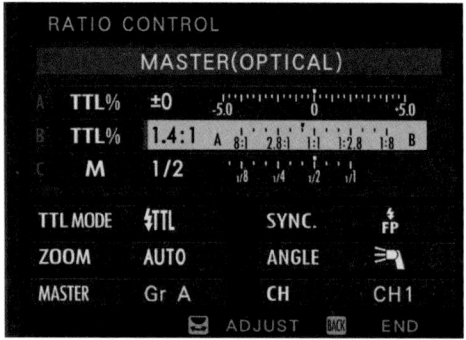

Fig. 73: In **TTL master mode,** one EF-X500 can control multiple flashguns in three independent groups (A, B, C) via a light communication protocol. Each group can be controlled via direct TTL, a ratio of another TTL group, or fully manually.

Many potential customers consider the EF-X500 disappointing, mostly because of the following reasons:

■ The EF-X500 was announced in January, 2016, yet ten months and several delays later, the flash still wasn't available.

■ The flash is quite large, heavy and expensive.

■ Wireless TTL control is realized with outdated light communication instead of state-of-the-art radio transmission.

■ Users have to buy and attach a heavy and expensive EF-X500 as a master controller to their camera.

There's hope that independent manufacturers will offer Fuji-compatible flash solutions with wireless radio TTL, multi-group support, and FP high-speed-sync in early 2017.

Generic third-party flash units	TIP 109

Basically, you can use any modern flashgun from any vendor with your X-T2, as long as you are prepared to manually set its power. You can connect third-party flash units directly to the camera's hot shoe, or use a cable or a wireless (radio) triggering device.

The camera's TTL modes aren't available when you are using third-party flashes because the camera isn't *metering* the flash light, it's only *triggering* the flash. Again, the maximum sync shutter speed is 1/250s. Unofficially, faster sync speeds may sometimes be possible.

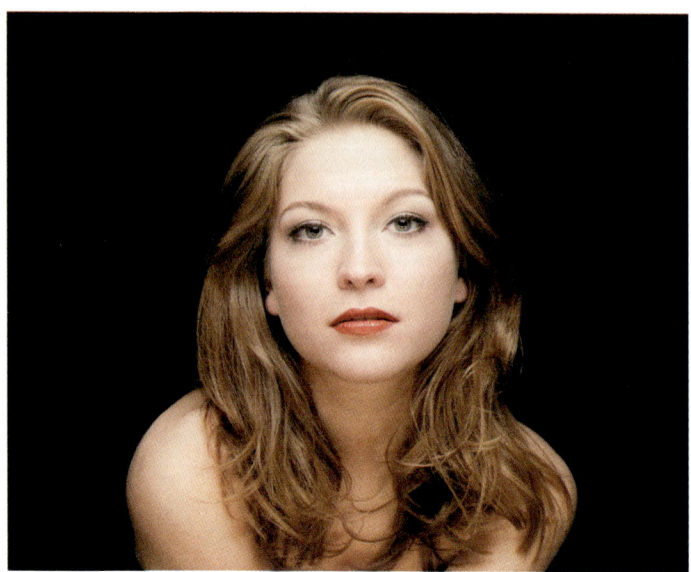

Fig. 74: Manually controlled **studio flash shot** using an Elinchrom Ranger Quadra.

Important: Attaching Canon-compatible TTL flash equipment to the hot-shoe of the X-T2 could result in the camera overheating and performing an emergency shutdown. While Fujifilm and Canon share the same the physical hot-shoe contacts, the protocols are not compatible. In this case, either tape-off the TTL contacts of your device or use an adapter that only loops the sync signal from the camera to the flash.

2.8 USING ADAPTED LENSES

Thanks to its short flange-back distance, the X-mount system is able to host almost every existing full-frame, medium format, cinema (Super 35 and larger), or APS-C lens. All you need is an appropriate adapter ring. This means that in addition to more than two dozen native lenses, you have access to hundreds of additional modern and legacy lenses.

Finding the right **lens adapter**	**TIP 110**

X-mount lens adapters are available for many old and current mounts. Here are a few tips to help you find the right adapter for your third-party lens:

■ Adapters are available at many price and quality levels, and you get what you pay for. Don't buy too cheap or you may end up buying twice. The German manufacturer Novoflex is setting the benchmark here, but their adapters can be more expensive than the lens you are adapting. Asian manufacturers like Kipon or Metabones enjoy a good reputation, and they all offer adapters for a wide variety of lens mounts.

■ Adapted lenses can only be used as manual focus lenses. There is currently no electronic adapter that can translate between Fuji's AF protocol and the AF protocols of popular brands like Canon or Nikon.

■ All adapted lenses use manual aperture settings and always operate with a manually set working aperture. This means that when you are stopping down the lens, the live view and live histogram of your X-T2 have to contend with the set aperture's reduced amount of light. It also means that adapted lenses can only be used in exposure modes **A** or **M**.

■ Many modern third-party lenses that don't feature a manual aperture ring can still be mechanically adapted to your X-T2, but you can't change their aperture while they are connected to your camera via an adapter. That's why some adapters feature a mechanical replacement aperture, but the results produced by these devices will differ from the results created by the original lens.

■ Modern electronic features like optical image stabilization (OIS) aren't supported since there is no communication between the X-T2 and the adapted lens. In fact, the camera believes that there's no lens attached at all.

- *Speed Booster Ultra* from Metabones offers an amazing possibility to attach full-frame lenses from Contax/Zeiss, Canon FD, Nikon G, Minolta MD, and Leica R to the X-T2 without changing their angle of view or cropping the image on your camera's APS-C sensor. Basically, your APS-C camera sees what a full-frame camera would see. Speed Booster is a focal reducer—basically the opposite of a teleconverter [70]. It reduces the focal length of the adapted lens by a factor of 0.71. At the same time, the brightness (speed) of the lens is increased by about one stop. At 400 to 600 dollars apiece, Speed Booster adapters aren't cheap. However, they offer better quality than knock-off products like the Lens Turbo II by Zhongyi Mitakon.

- Fujifilm offers its own adapter for Leica M-type full-frame lenses. This is a regular adapter (no Speed Booster), but it features electronic contacts so the camera will recognize it. It also features an Fn button that provides direct access to the camera's MOUNT ADAPTOR SETTING menu. With all other adapters, you have to set SET UP > BUTTON/DIAL SETTING > SHOOT WITHOUT LENS > ON in order to take a picture.

- Caution: don't use cheap macro lens adapters with electronic contacts. These cheap adapters are designed to serve as macro spacer rings for native X-mount lenses. They promise full AF functionality thanks to their electronic X-mount contacts, but in reality, these adapter rings can be a bad fit and can damage your camera and lenses. Instead, I recommend using Fuji's own electronic macro extension tubes MCEX-11 and MCEX-16.

- Never try to combine more than one adapter. Stacking adapters leads to a measurable and visible loss in quality. Instead, get the right adapter for your lens.

| Adapting third-party lenses: here's how… | TIP 111 |

When you connect third-party lenses to your camera via an adapter, the camera won't notice it due to the lack of electronic contacts. The X-T2 will think there's no lens attached at all. The only exception is using Fuji's own Leica M-mount adapter.

■ In order to make the camera work with adapted lenses, set SET UP > BUTTON/DIAL SETTING > SHOOT WITHOUT LENS > ON.

■ Enter the focal length of your adapted lens in the SHOOTING SETTING > MOUNT ADAPTOR SETTING > LENS REGISTRATION menu. You can either select the focal length from one of four presets or enter it manually in LENS 5 or LENS 6. Always enter the actual focal length of a lens (as it is printed on the lens), not its full-frame equivalent for APS-C cameras. This ensures that the EXIF data will display the correct focal length.

| Exposing with adapted lenses | TIP 112 |

Adapted lenses can be used in exposure modes **A** (aperture priority) and **M** (manual mode). There are also a few notable differences between exposing with native lenses and adapted lenses:

■ Native lenses close to working aperture only when the shutter is half-pressed or when the shot is actually taken. Adapted lenses always operate with the aperture set by the user. As soon as you stop down an adapted lens, less light reaches the sensor and the camera's exposure metering. Stopping down adapted lenses increases the depth of field in the viewfinder.

- Since less light reaches the sensor, the camera has to more strongly amplify the live view image in order to display an accurate WYSIWYG simulation of the scene. This decreases the quality of the live view image and can also negatively affect the live view's frame rate.

- Since the camera thinks there's no lens attached at all, the aperture is always displayed as F0 in the viewfinder. There's no way for the camera to know which aperture has actually been set on an adapted lens.

- Shooting in poor light with adapted lenses can be tricky when you stop down the aperture. It's easy to reach the live view's amplification limit. Once this limit is reached, the live view and live histogram cannot display the actual brightness of the scene, so it appears darker than the image that will be actually exposed. However, exposure metering will still work correctly and the camera will display the correct shutter speed. In mode **M**, the ±3 EV light scale in the display will also work correctly.

- Since the electronic live view cannot control the aperture of an adapted lens, it takes longer for the camera to adjust to abrupt brightness changes. You can test this yourself by quickly panning the camera from a bright scene to a dark scene and vice versa. With adapted lenses, the camera will need a few seconds for the live view to adapt to the changing brightness levels.

TIP 113	Focusing with adapted lenses

Adapted lenses can only be focused manually. Here are a few tips to make things easier for you:

- Set the focus selector of your X-T2 to manual focus. This makes sure that MF assistants such as focus check, focus peaking, and digital split image are available.

- The electronic distance and depth-of-field (DOF) scale of your X-T2 is useless in concert with adapted lenses. Instead, you have to rely on analog scales and markers that may be engraved in the barrel of your adapted lens. Remember that the DOF scale on your lens is probably less conservative than what you're used to from the electronic scale in your X-T2. The analog scale doesn't guarantee pixel-sharp results at 100% magnification. Instead, it will more likely resemble the FILM FORMAT BASIS option of the X-T2's electronic DOF scale.

- The most important tool for focusing with adapted lenses is the magnifier tool. You can activate it by pressing the rear command dial. Turn the rear command dial to cycle between two available magnifications. Don't forget: instead of focusing and recomposing, it's better to select a focus frame that covers the part of the image you want to be in focus. You can move the focus frame with the focus stick.

- Use focus peaking or digital split image. You can cycle between these MF assistants and the standard view by pressing and holding the rear command dial. The magnifier tool can be combined with focus peaking and digital split image. However, in concert with digital split image, only one magnification level is available.

- The magnifier tool and MF assistants work best at wide-open aperture, when the DOF is as small as possible. However, some lenses exhibit focus shift, meaning the focus plane shifts backward when the lens is stopped down. The increased DOF from stopping down the lens may not be sufficient to compensate for the focus shift, so your carefully focused shot will end up out of focus when the aperture is closed. If you are using a lens with pronounced focus shift, it's better to focus with the actual working aperture instead of the wide-open aperture.

Please note that focus shift isn't a matter of price—even a few high-end lenses from Leica and Zeiss suffer from it.

TIP 114	Using the **Fujifilm M-mount adapter**

Fuji's own M-mount adapter is a little bit different from conventional adapters:

- The adapter features electronic XF lens contacts to identify itself to the camera. However, there's no transmission of any lens data since the adapter doesn't know which M-type lens has been attached or what distance and aperture has been set. Sadly, the electronic contacts also make the inner adapter tube thinner than normal, so not all M-type lenses are physically compatible with it. This website [71] has a list of compatible and incompatible lenses. Fuji also encloses a template with its M adapter that you can use to find out if your M lens measures up with the adapter.

- Pressing the function button on the adapter directly opens the camera's adapter menu.

- The adapter menu offers a few additional functions when a Fuji M-mount adapter is attached. In addition to entering the focal length, you can also enter correction values for lens distortion, color shading, and vignetting. Those corrections only affect the JPEGs during RAW conversion with the built-in or external RAW converters. As usual, the corrections are burned into the RAW file metadata where they can be interpreted by RAW conversion software. However, color-shade data is currently only processed by the camera's built-in converter. For each adapted lens, you have to find out the right correction values for yourself before you can enter them. There aren't any reference lists you can use that I know of.

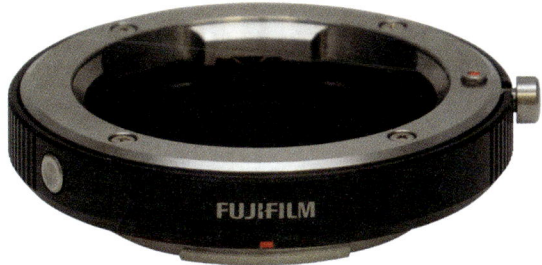

Fig. 75: Fujifilm's own **M-mount adapter** features electronic contacts and a function button that opens the camera's adapter menu.

| Quality considerations | **TIP 115** |

Pixel peeping is en vogue, but many classic lenses rooted in the area of analog film weren't made for high-resolution digital sensors. While some very expensive Leica lenses may be outright disappointing when used on an X-T2, some really cheap old lenses can deliver excellent results.

How can we explain that?

The lens design plays a major role. Some compact lenses (typically for M-mount cameras) feature a symmetrical design that tends to be more problematic with digital sensors than telecentric SLR designs.

Also note that most adapted lenses are intended for full-frame [72] cameras. Attached to an X-T2 with its smaller APS-C [73] sensor (23,7×15,6 mm), the format of the lens is cropped. If you could extend the size of Fuji's older 16MP APS-C sensor to full-frame (36×24mm), its resolution would be 36 megapixels, just like the Nikon D810 or Sony's A7r. Obviously, there aren't many older full-frame lenses that can actually use this kind of resolution. Instead, many older lenses offer something else: character. Because maximum sharpness and resolution weren't as important then as they are today, the designers of legacy lenses could put their priorities elsewhere, for example by designing lenses that provide outstanding bokeh [74].

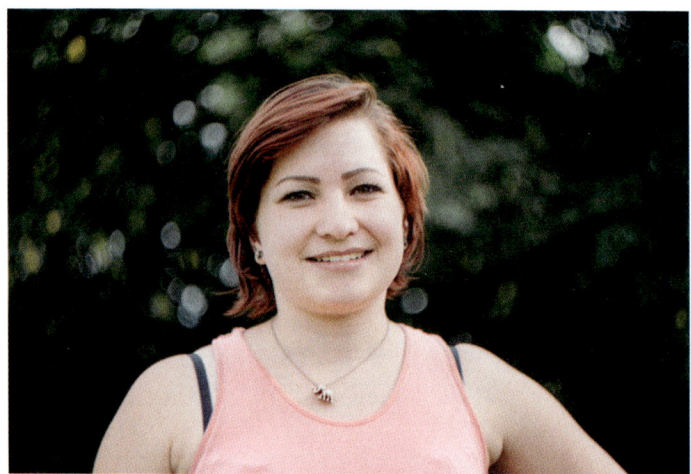

Fig. 76: Good legacy lenses don't have to be expensive: this shot was taken with a Russian **Helios 44M-4,** a 58mmF2 lens with an M42 screw-mount. You can often find this lens online for less than 25 dollars.

TIP 116	**Speed Booster:** miracle or trick?

Speed Booster and Speed Booster Ultra from Metabones are very special adapters. They convert the focal lengths of full-frame lenses to their APS-C equivalents. This means that the adapted lens covers the same angle of view on your X-T2 as it would on a full-frame camera.

Take my *Carl Zeiss Sonnar T* 2.8/180 MM* as an example. It's a classic telephoto lens with a Contax/Yashica full-frame mount. Adapting this lens to my X-T2 *without* Speed Booster causes the results to look like images taken with a 270mmF4.2 lens on a full-frame camera. That's because there is a crop factor of 1.5 between full-frame and APS-C.

Of course, many users of full-frame lenses would like to use them on a smaller APS-C camera like the X-T2, yet keep the angle of view and depth of field constant. Speed Booster can do that for you because it reduces the focal length of the adapted lens by a factor of 0.71. With Speed Booster, my 2.8/180mm full-frame Sonnar turns into a 2/128mm APS-C lens.

Is there a price to pay? Well, yes, since Speed Booster isn't cheap. With regards to image quality, the MTF [75] of the new lens is actually improved, but there's a chance of vignetting when Speed Booster is used to adapt fast lenses. That said, the new Speed Booster Ultra improves vignetting issues that were problematic with the original Speed Booster. In any case, it's better than knock-off products such as Lens Turbo II.

Speed Booster increases the speed (or maximum aperture) of a lens by about one stop, so you can use faster shutter speeds or lower ISO settings. For example, let's assume you need ISO 800 to shoot a scene with your full-frame DSLR at f/2.8 (wide open) with a 180mm lens and 1/1000s. On the X-T2, Speed Booster turns this lens into a 128mmF2 lens with the same angle of view. Shooting wide open (now f/2) at 1/1000s, you can drop the ISO to 400. Since full-frame sensors tend to offer an ISO advantage of about one stop over APS-C, the results from both cameras should be equivalent, because the X-T2 sensor can compensate its smaller size by applying 1 EV less ISO amplification.

Speed Booster is available for several classic mounts, such as Canon FD, Nikon G, Contax/Yashica (Zeiss), Minolta MD, Contarex, ALPA, and Leica R. Sadly, there is no Speed Booster for Leica M, because an M adapter would be too thin to house the necessary optics.

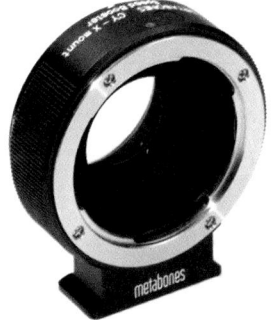

Fig. 77: Metabones **Speed Booster** with Contax mount

2.9 WIRELESS REMOTE CONTROL AND TETHERING

Fuji's own Camera Remote app works with wireless iOS and Android devices, and it allows you to remotely control your camera by providing a live view image and a touch-screen interface to set the focus point, change exposure parameters, and take a shot.

TIP 117	Using the **Camera Remote App**

Camera Remote allows you to control the X-T2 from an Android or iOS device running Fuji's Cam Remote app. The wireless connection is based on the camera's or smart-phone's Wi-fi capabilities.

In order to use Camera Remote, you have to download and install the free Cam Remote app on your smartphone or tablet. You can find download links, instructions, and additional information at this website [76].

*Important: Make sure you use the **Cam Remote App** and not the older **Camera App**.*

Here's how Camera Remote works with iOS devices (it shouldn't be much different for Android users):

■ Select SHOOTING SETTING > WIRELESS COMMUNI-CATION on your camera. The X-T2 now enters wireless mode and emits a Wi-fi signal.

■ Hook up your smartphone's or tablet's Wi-fi with the camera's Wi-fi network. Each camera comes with a unique network name that you can customize in SET UP > CONNECTION SETTING > WIRELESS SETTINGS > GENERAL SETTINGS > NAME.

- Open the Cam Remote app and select Remote Control. The mobile device will now assume control over the camera and display a live view image along with options to adjust shutter speed, aperture or exposure compensation. There's also a virtual shutter button and a small shooting menu that allows you to adjust parameters like ISO, film simulation, white balance, macro, flash mode, or self-timer.

- In order to autofocus on a specific part of the live view image, double-tap with your finger on it. Focus will be confirmed with a green rectangle, and the camera will issue a confirmation beep. If no focus lock can be established, the rectangle will appear in red.

- Adjust your exposure parameters as required. The brightness of the live view will change accordingly. Please note that there's no live histogram.

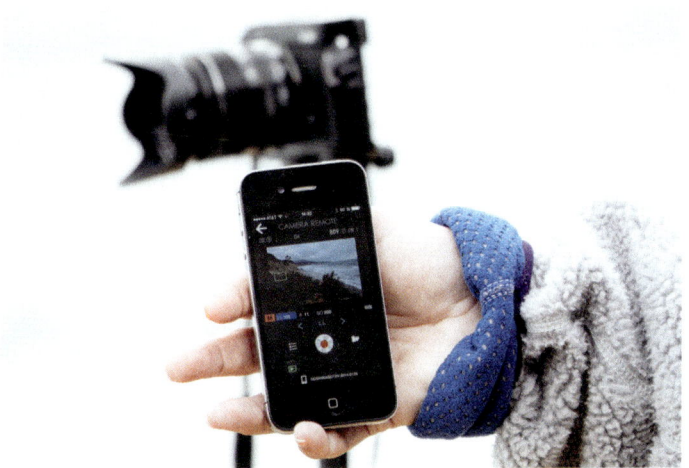

Fig. 78: **Camera Remote** offers a simple interface to control your camera with a smartphone or tablet. To autofocus, double-tap on a specific part of the WYSIWYG live view and wait for the green confirmation rectangle to appear. Sadly, there is no live histogram, and you can't magnify the live view. There is a rudimentary shooting menu, a virtual shutter button, and a playback button that allows you to review images and transfer JPEGs to your mobile device.

Here are a few things you might want to know about Camera Remote:

- Fuji's Camera Remote app allows you to adjust exposure parameters (aperture, shutter speed, ISO, exposure compensation), but you can't remotely change the camera's exposure mode. This means that you have to manually set the camera to either **P**, **A**, **S**, or **M** mode *before* you select WIRELESS COMMUNICATION in the camera menu. In order to change the exposure mode during remote shooting, you have to first disconnect Camera Remote, make the desired changes in the camera, and then start over with a new connection as directed above.

- There's no electronic level indicator and no live histogram in the Camera Remote live view on your mobile device.

- You can change several shooting parameters from within the Camera Remote app (ISO, film simulation, white balance preset, macro, flash mode, self-timer), but other parameters (such as dynamic range or Auto-ISO minimum shutter speed) have to be preset in the camera before entering wireless communication mode.

- There is no bulb functionality in Camera Remote, so your maximum exposure time is limited to the extent of the T setting. If you need more, better use a conventional (tethered or wireless) remote shutter release.

- The X-T2 also allows you to shoot video with Camera Remote.

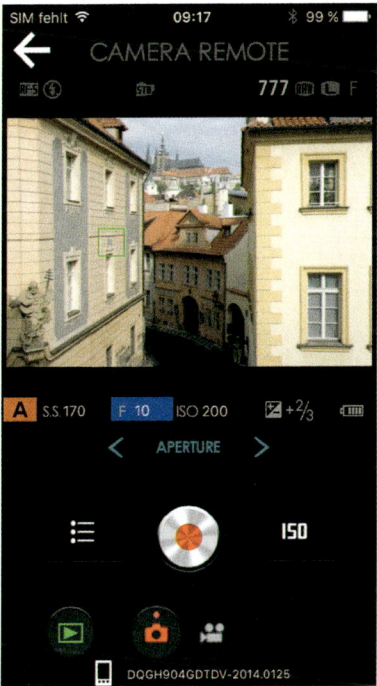

Fig. 79: Changing exposure parameters affects the WYSIWYG live view. The live view always reflects the currently selected film simulation and JPEG parameters. Like in the X-T2 itself, there is a preview of manually selected DR settings (DR200%, DR400%).

A few more tips and hints:

■ I use Camera Remote mostly in manual exposure mode **M**; I feel that this is the most convenient and efficient way to adjust shooting parameters. Changing a parameter (shutter speed, aperture, ISO) immediately adjusts the live view brightness.

■ iOS users may be annoyed by the need to frequently reconnect the smartphone to the camera's Wi-fi network, since the connection has to be dropped and reestablished for every mode or parameter change made in the camera. This can be particularly cumbersome at home, where the iOS device is automatically reconnecting with your home network as soon as the camera has been disconnected.

■ Some users may suffer from connection losses caused by interfering networks that are transmitting on the same Wi-fi channel as the camera. Sadly, there is currently no way to change the camera's transmission channel.

■ In order to transfer JPEGs from the camera to your mobile device with full 24MP resolution, make sure to select SET UP > CONNECTION SETTING > WIRELESS SETTINGS > RESIZE IMAGE FOR SMARTPHONE > OFF. Otherwise, the transferred images will be downsized to 3 megapixels.

■ Manual DR extension settings (DR200%, DR400%) are reflected in the Camera Remote live view of the X-T2. So are JPEG parameters such as contrast (HIGHLIGHT TONE, SHADOW TONE) or white balance settings, and in manual mode **M**, the Camera Remote live view will also respect any settings made in SET UP > SCREEN SET-UP > PREVIEW EXP./WB IN MANUAL MODE.

■ Wi-fi drains the battery, so you better pack spare batteries or use Fuji's CP-W126 DC [77] DC coupler and AC-9V [78] power adapter to connect the X-T2 to an external power source. If you use the Vertical Power Booster Grip, you can power the camera directly with the supplied charger, or plug an AC-9V into the grip.

Besides remote controlling [79] the X-T2, the Camera Remote app offers additional functions that allow you to transfer JPEGs from the camera to your mobile device (one by one [80] or in groups [81]) and to copy GPS location data [82] from your smartphone or tablet to the camera.

| TIP 118 | Streaming the live view via HDMI |

The X-T2 is Fujifilm's first camera to offer HDMI live-streaming, meaning that the contents of the live view (viewfinder or LCD) can be transmitted to a monitor, TV, or beamer via the camera's HDMI connection. All you have to do is connect the camera's Micro-HDMI jack to a suitable monitor with a digital input (HDMI, DVI, etc.). Real-time streaming will start automatically once the connection is established.

This is a very useful feature for workshops, product demonstrations or professional productions, where customers can see on a monitor what the photographer is seeing in the live view.

You can also use the HDMI live view output to connect the camera to an HD frame-grabber which is in turn connected to your computer. With this setup, you can make video recordings and screenshots of the live view.

Tethered shooting via USB	TIP 119

Tethered shooting involves controlling the camera via a computer that is connected (tethered) to the camera via a USB 3 or USB 2 cable.

In order to use the X-T2 for tethering, you must use firmware version 1.10 or later on your camera and select either USB AUTO or USB FIXED in the SET UP > CONNECTION SETTING > PC SHOOT MODE menu. That way, the X-T2 is either recognizing (AUTO) or even forcing (FIXED) a computer connection via USB, yielding control to compatible tethering software on the computer

There are two basic PC software options you can use to tether your X-T2:

- **HS-V5** (version 1.3 or later) is a Windows-only software from Fujifilm that allows remote shooting via USB. It's noteworthy that the new version only offers basic controls of the X-T2, so users who already know HS-V5 from tethering their X-T1 may be disappointed to learn that they are losing at least ¾ of the previous functionality. Don't worry, though: What's missing in HS-V5 has been added to the Tether Shooting Plug-in PRO for Adobe Lightroom. HS-V5 can be purchased from Fujifilm or where Fujifilm cameras are sold. If you are already using the older version 1.2 of HS-V5 with an X-T1, get the free update to version 1.3.

■ The **Tether Shooting Plug-in PRO for Adobe Lightroom** is a new macOS and Windows plug-in for Lightroom users. It's a $79 download from Adobe [83]. The Pro version of this plug-in supports a live view image on your computer and offers controls for most camera functions. There's also a basic version of the plug-in, and owners of an older Lightroom tether plug-in for the X-T1 (plug-in version 1.2) can get a free update to the basic plug-in version 1.3 (which supports the X-T2). However, to get access to controls that go beyond releasing the shutter, you will have to get the new Pro plug-in. The good news is that the Pro plug-in also supports the X-T1, so you don't have to purchase or use different plug-ins if you are using both models.

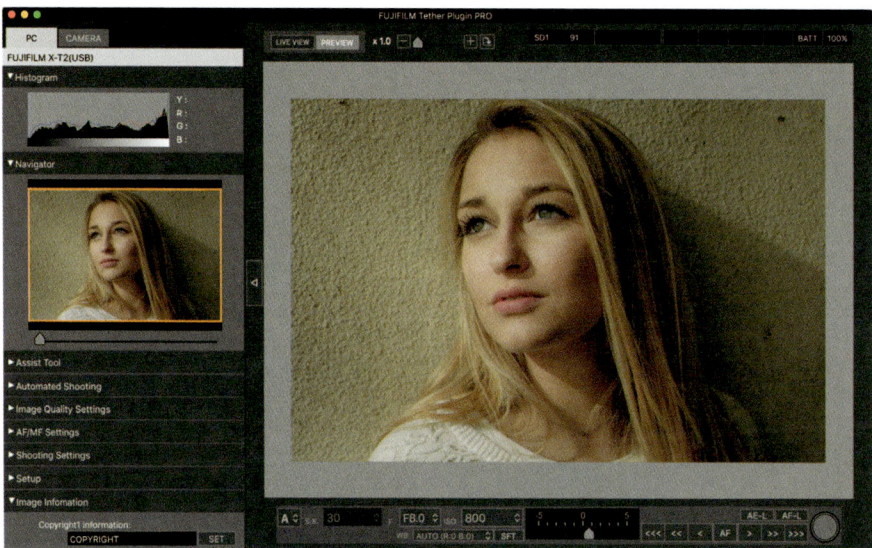

Fig. 80: The new Tether Shooting Plug-in PRO for Adobe Lightroom supports the X-T1 and X-T2 and offers a live view image and comprehensive control over the camera. New features include color histograms, focus stacking, expanded bracketing, and the possibility to enter copyright information. You can also save and load full camera configurations.

2.10 ANYTHING ELSE?

Hopefully, this book was able to answer many of your questions that went beyond the manual of your camera. However, this isn't the end: you can read my *X-Pert Corner* blog, participate in Fuji X forums, or join one of my Fuji X Secrets workshops.

Forums, blogs, and workshops: be a part of it!	TIP 120

- High-resolution versions of selected images in this book are available in this Flickr album [84].

- At Fuji X Secrets [64], you will find articles and updates for this book that cover new firmware features. You might also be interested in reading my X-T2 first look review [85], as it contains additional information and examples explaining the X-T2's capabilities.

- My free X-Pert Corner blog covers a variety of topics about the Fujifilm X series. You will find everything from service articles that go beyond this book to First Look previews of new cameras and lenses. You can read X-Pert Corner here [86].

- There are several online forums that focus on Fujifilm's X series: The Original Fuji X Forum [87]; The Ultimate Fuji X Forum [88]; the Fuji X-Series Forum[89]; and FujiXSpot [90]. The latter forum contains a special section where I'm personally available to answer questions or discuss Fuji X-related issues. Please use this forum to contact me with questions or comments.

- Books, blogs, and forums are great, but what about a more personal touch? My site Fuji X Secrets [64] offers a series of advanced workshops for Fuji X-series users. My workshops cover topics that are similar to those in this book, but on a more in-depth and comprehensive level, including practical demonstrations and plenty of sample images. We work in small groups, and our delegates set the agenda. It's everything you always wanted to know about X, but were afraid to ask. We are also organizing travel workshops to great photo locations: In 2015, we went to Istanbul, and in November 2016, we hosted an exclusive week-long Fuji X Secrets Ultimate workshop in Phuket, Thailand. In late May 2017, we are going to Guernsey (Channel Islands), and for November 2017, we plan an exclusive Fuji X Secrets travel workshop in New Zealand.

ONLINE REFERENCES

Websites are not run by Rocky Nook, and are subject to change without our knowledge.

If necessary, we will update these references. For an updated version of this reference list, please download the available document at:

http://www.rockynook.com/fujifilm-x-t2-online-references/

[01] http://www.fujifilm.com/support/digital_cameras/manuals/

[02] http://www.apple.com/shop/product/MD837AM/A/apple-world-travel-adapter-kit?fnode=3c

[03] http://www.fujifilm.com/support/digital_cameras/software/

[04] http://digital-cameras.support.fujifilm.com/app/answers/detail/a_id/19061/kw/firmware/p/43/c/1524

[05] http://digital-cameras.support.fujifilm.com/app/answers/detail/a_id/18998/kw/firmware/p/43/c/1524

[06] http://digital-cameras.support.fujifilm.com/app/answers/detail/a_id/18997/kw/firmware/p/43/c/1524

[07] http://www.fujifilm.com/products/digital_cameras/x/fujifilm_x_t2/features/page_06.html

[08] https://en.wikipedia.org/wiki/Live_preview

[09] https://en.wikipedia.org/wiki/Crop_factor

[10] https://en.wikipedia.org/wiki/Image_stabilization

[11] https://en.wikipedia.org/wiki/Motion_blur

[12] https://en.wikipedia.org/wiki/Panning_(camera)

[13] https://en.wikipedia.org/wiki/Circle_of_confusion

[14] http://www.cambridgeincolour.com/tutorials/diffraction-photography.htm

[15] https://en.wikipedia.org/wiki/Deconvolution

[16] https://en.wikipedia.org/wiki/Vignetting

[17] https://en.wikipedia.org/wiki/Distortion_(optics)

[18] https://en.wikipedia.org/wiki/Chromatic_aberration

[19] http://www.triggertrap.com

[20] http://app.fujifilm-dsc.com/en/camera_remote/index.html

[21] https://en.wikipedia.org/wiki/Exchangeable_image_file_format

[22] https://en.wikipedia.org/wiki/Dark-frame_subtraction

[23]   https://en.wikipedia.org/wiki/Raw_image_format

[24]   https://en.wikipedia.org/wiki/WYSIWYG

[25]   https://en.wikipedia.org/wiki/Live_preview

[26]   https://en.wikipedia.org/wiki/Zone_System

[27]   https://en.wikipedia.org/wiki/Depth_of_field

[28]   https://en.wikipedia.org/wiki/Aperture_priority

[29]   https://en.wikipedia.org/wiki/Aperture

[30]   https://en.wikipedia.org/wiki/Shutter_priority

[31]   https://en.wikipedia.org/wiki/Shutter_speed

[32]   https://en.wikipedia.org/wiki/Long-exposure_photography

[33]   http://www.cambridgeincolour.com/tutorials/camera-shake.htm

[34]   http://www.completedigitalphotography.com/?p=510

[35]   https://en.wikipedia.org/wiki/Bracketing

[36]   https://en.wikipedia.org/wiki/Neutral-density_filter

[37]   https://en.wikipedia.org/wiki/Film_speed#Standard_output_sensitivity_.28SOS.29

[38]   https://www.flickr.com/gp/ricopfirstinger/u657cM

[39]   http://www.fujirumors.com/using-auto-iso/

[40]   http://www.diyphotography.net/lighting-high-key-and-low-key/

[41]   https://en.wikipedia.org/wiki/High-dynamic-range_imaging

[42]   https://en.wikipedia.org/wiki/Rolling_shutter

[43]   http://digital-photography-school.com/the-problem-with-the-focus-recompose-method/

[44]   http://www.fujifilm-x.com/af/en/

[45]   http://www.fujirumors.com/using-firmware-4/

[46]   https://en.wikipedia.org/wiki/Hyperfocal_distance

[47]   https://www.youtube.com/watch?v=7FR3l6S12JA

[48]   http://www.cambridgeincolour.com/tutorials/hyperfocal-distance.htm

[49]   http://www.fujifilm.com/products/digital_cameras/accessories/pdf/mcex_01.pdf

[50]   http://www.cambridgeincolour.com/tutorials/white-balance.htm

[51]   https://en.wikipedia.org/wiki/Gray_card

[52]   https://en.wikipedia.org/wiki/Contrast_(vision)

[53]   https://en.wikipedia.org/wiki/Colorfulness

[54]   https://en.wikipedia.org/wiki/Color_space

[55]   https://en.wikipedia.org/wiki/srgb_color_space

[56]   https://en.wikipedia.org/wiki/Adobe_RGB_color_space

[57]   https://en.wikipedia.org/wiki/Gamut

[58]   https://silkypix.isl.co.jp/en/

[59] http://www.fujifilm.com/support/digital_cameras/software/myfinepix_studio/rfc/

[60] http://www.adobe.com/products/photoshop-lightroom.html

[61] https://www.phaseone.com/en/Products/Software/Capture-One-Pro/Highlights.aspx

[62] http://www.iridientdigital.com

[63] http://www.picturecode.com

[64] https://fuji-x-secrets.net/

[65] http://www.fujifilm.com/support/digital_cameras/software/lut/

[66] https://en.wikipedia.org/wiki/Through-the-lens_metering#Through_the_lens_flash_metering

[67] https://en.wikipedia.org/wiki/Flash_synchronization

[68] https://en.wikipedia.org/wiki/Red-eye_effect

[69] https://en.wikipedia.org/wiki/Catch_light

[70] https://en.wikipedia.org/wiki/Teleconverter

[71] http://www.fujifilm.com/products/digital_cameras/accessories/lens/mount/fujifilm_m_mount_adapter/compatibility_chart/index.html

[72] https://en.wikipedia.org/wiki/135_film

[73] https://en.wikipedia.org/wiki/APS-C

[74] https://en.wikipedia.org/wiki/Bokeh

[75] https://en.wikipedia.org/wiki/Optical_transfer_function

[76] http://app.fujifilm-dsc.com/en/camera_remote/index.html

[77] http://www.fujifilm.com/products/digital_cameras/accessories/batteries/#coupler

[78] http://www.fujifilm.com/products/digital_cameras/accessories/batteries/#adapter

[79] http://app.fujifilm-dsc.com/en/camera_remote/guide05.html

[80] http://app.fujifilm-dsc.com/en/camera_remote/guide01.html

[81] http://app.fujifilm-dsc.com/en/camera_remote/guide03.html

[82] http://app.fujifilm-dsc.com/en/camera_remote/guide02.html

[83] https://creative.adobe.com/addons/products/16759

[84] https://www.flickr.com/gp/ricopfirstinger/u657cM

[85] https://fuji-x-secrets.net/2016/07/25/first-look-review-fujifilm-x-t2/

[86] http://www.fujirumors.com/category/x-pert/

[87] http://www.fujix-forum.com

[88] http://www.fuji-x-forum.com

[89] http://www.fujixseries.com

[90] https://www.fujixspot.com

INDEX